Curriculum
s p a c e s

A Book Series of
Curriculum Studies

William F. Pinar
General Editor

VOLUME 16

PETER LANG
New York • Washington, D.C./Baltimore • Bern
Frankfurt am Main • Berlin • Brussels • Vienna • Oxford

Lisa J. Cary

Curriculum
spaces

Discourse, Postmodern Theory
and Educational Research

PETER LANG
New York • Washington, D.C./Baltimore • Bern
Frankfurt am Main • Berlin • Brussels • Vienna • Oxford

Library of Congress Cataloging-in-Publication Data

Cary, Lisa J.
Curriculum spaces: discourse, postmodern theory
and educational research / Lisa J. Cary.
p. cm. — (Complicated conversation; v. 16)
Includes bibliographical references and index.
1. Education—Curricula. 2. Postmodernism and education.
3. Education—Research. I. Title. II. Series.
LB1570.C266   375.0001—dc22   2006004966
ISBN 978-0-8204-8128-9
ISSN 1534-2816

Bibliographic information published by **Die Deutsche Bibliothek**.
Die Deutsche Bibliothek lists this publication in the "Deutsche
Nationalbibliografie"; detailed bibliographic data is available
on the Internet at http://dnb.ddb.de/.

Cover design by Lisa Barfield
Cover photo by Lisa J. Cary
Author photo by Floyd B. Ausburn

The paper in this book meets the guidelines for permanence and durability
of the Committee on Production Guidelines for Book Longevity
of the Council of Library Resources.

© 2007, 2006 Peter Lang Publishing, Inc., New York
29 Broadway, 18th floor, New York, NY 10006
www.peterlang.com

All rights reserved.
Reprint or reproduction, even partially, in all forms such as microfilm,
xerography, microfiche, microcard, and offset strictly prohibited.

Printed in the United States of America

This book is dedicated to my family.

Contents

Foreword	Arrivals and Departures	ix
Chapter 1	**Curriculum Spaces Research Theory**	1
	The Crisis of Representation	4
	Epistemology	5
	Postmodern Theories	8
	Critical Discourse Analysis	15
	Conclusion	19
Chapter 2	**The Methodological Journey**	21
	Life History—Revisiting Irene	22
	Extending Ethnography	35
	Positionality	50
	Final Thoughts	54
Chapter 3	**The Good Teacher: Charter Schools and Teacher Education**	57
	A Postmodern Moment	59
	Social and Educational Discourses	61
	Teacher Education Reform Rhetoric—The Professional Development School Model	62
	The Charter School for 'Push-Out Recovery'	69
	Redemptive Cultures	76
Chapter 4	**Gender and Race: Discourses That Other**	79
	Constructing Gender	79
	Critical Discourse Analysis and Deviant Historiography	82
	Constructing Discourses of the Deviant Female Juvenile Offender	83
	The Juvenile Justice System	91

	Theorizing the Raced Construction of the Subject in Multicultural Education	97
	Spaces of Othering through Gender and Race	103
Chapter 5	**A Postcolonial Subject Position**	105
	9/11 Otherness	105
	Colonized and Colonizing Spaces	107
	Citizens and Aliens	109
	A Postcolonial Story	111
	At Home—Theoretically Speaking	115
	Postscript	118
Chapter 6	**The Hollywood Teacher: Knowing through Film**	121
	Redemptive Spaces and Youth in Trouble	122
	Vintage Films	123
	The Perfect Teacher—Mr. Chips	124
	The Anti-Teacher—Miss Jean Brodie	126
	A Psychoanalytic Moment	129
	So What?	131
Chapter 7	**From Currere to Curriculum Spaces**	133
	Where Do We Go From Here?	136
	Ethics	137
Bibliography		139
Index		151

Foreword
Arrivals and Departures

I have been thinking a lot lately about the arrivals that intersect at this point in my life. It seems we never "arrive"—rather, we are always already engaged in multiple arrivals (mirroring the hours spent in airports on this journey of arrivals and departures). The book you are about to read is a representation of the journey from teacher to researcher/ theorist that began twelve years ago when I left Australia. In Australia, to this day, I am a teacher. For two years in Canada, I was a graduate student of a master's degree in Curriculum and Instruction and a teacher as I lectured in teaching methods. I lived in a prairie city and experienced a coldness I shall never forget—only matched by the warmth of the people. And then, I came to the United States of America and during my time in this country, ten years, I have been seduced by the consumer life and disturbed by the myths of democracy.

I came to this country, the USA, as a teacher and student. I was an experienced professional and I entered a doctoral program at a large Midwest research university where a reform movement in teacher education dominated how we 'knew' teaching. This included attempting to erase the historic contribution of women and a valorization of a male model of knowing—all in an attempt to increase the professional standing of the vocation. It also valorized practice over theory. I was very concerned. As a result, I focused my dissertation research on that topic and began to become a researcher. Interestingly enough, my doctoral studies coalesced into a sort of Curriculum Studies double major with Social Studies/Global Education and Cultural Studies in Education. I found my concerns with the exclusive discourses of citizenship in Social Studies/Global Education coupled with the high theory and postmodern position of Cultural Studies (based on the Birmingham School of Cultural Studies) made it possible to think differently about education. I was able to focus not only on a subject area, but also on issues of research and epistemology, framed by various theoretical positions including poststructural feminism, postcolonial studies, psychoanalytic theory and critical theory. You can see the results of these intersections in this book.

In chapter one, I bring together the various theories about how ways of knowing are framed—epistemological theories. My research life now focuses on understanding how exclusion works—hence this book. It is all about how some bodies, actions, beliefs and experiences are legitimized as normal and acceptable (possible) and others are abnormal, deviant and unacceptable (impossible). I outline the approach I call *Curriculum Spaces Research Theory*. Finally, I present a number of suggestions and ideas for utilizing this approach.

The second chapter presents the methodological journey of the development of this research theory. This work is unique because it brings together curriculum theory (as discussed in chapter one) and research theory. Therefore, in chapter two I outline my initial concerns with the limits of methodology as they emerged within my master's thesis using Life History methodology. I then discuss the way I used Postmodern Ethnography to reveal and highlight how culture travels and issues of home and field in my doctoral dissertation work studying the Professional Development School model. It is important to note that the frequent failure of in-depth data analysis evident in educational research is a main concern that has led me to provide this analytical research theory that can be applied to data collected using any methodology.

Chapters three through five provide discussions of exemplars of the Curriculum Spaces Research Theory. I have created departures for theory building using both traditional school subjects (Social Studies Education—Citizenship and Teacher education discourses) and contemporary social issues (9/11). For example, in chapter three I suggest it is important to begin with social and educational discourses that frame subject positions, because the 'big picture' is often left out. Understanding how *the way we know* teacher education and multicultural education are framed by masculine frames and White curriculum spaces is also addressed. This knowing in teacher education has historically highlighted a move toward a gendered salvation of teacher education—a move away from the historically feminized profession toward a more masculine, scientific, technical model. And even the best of intentions of Multicultural Education at the societal level can be critiqued as assimilationist and White.

Although the three levels of discursive production (societal, institutional and local) of knowing are separated in these chapters, they are blurred and intersect in the way we know. However, in chapter four I focus on a research project topic that is very revealing about how power plays out in the dominant social constructions of the particular subject position of woman in the total institution. In this case, female juvenile offenders are unwomanly and seen as a threat to society—or so the construction of this epistemological space has been produced through historical, social and cultural influences. They are thus a failure and outcast. Therefore, the way we know them can teach us a lot about how the effects of power play out on the bodies of individuals, excluded and erased in educational institutions.

Chapter five takes us to the personal or local level. Over the last few years as I have been struggling with my response to 9/11 I found my understanding of postcolonial theory highlighted an issue of space that could be supported through other theories. Issues framing how we know the 'good teacher' are discussed in chapters three and six. I discuss a study of a charter school for drop-outs—or, as they prefer, a 'push-out recovery program' in chapter three and then present a brief study of films about teachers and the reflections of populist thought on what a teacher 'should be' as well as a way to think about the production of the epistemological space of being 'a good teacher' in chapter six. A number of fascinating issues of discipline, sexualized knowing, gender and race appear in these seemingly harmless Hollywood representations. I use a lot of film in my classes and it is a sign of 'settling into my space' that I am now able (or legitimate enough) to bring my teacher self together with my researcher self.

As a result, in the final chapter, chapter seven, I revisit what I call a 'research theory' to the study of curriculum issues. This calls for an understanding at all times that curriculum is more than a textbook, more than a classroom and more than teachers and students. It is all the social influences, populist crises, military campaigns and historical moments that shape our lives—when we are in school and in our lives beyond the classroom. Historically, moves and counter-moves to define curriculum have occurred within highly contested terrain. The position taken in this book is a move to study curriculum as a discursively produced historically, socially, politically and economically inscribed epistemological space. Therefore, I put forward this approach as one way to understand how we know what we know. It is an epistemological approach to study the knowing subject and researcher positionality. This book presents a three-pronged approach—bringing together curriculum theory, educational research theory and exemplars of research projects.

I suggest here that we consider the arrivals and departures in our lives in order to highlight that we can never arrive, rather we are always arriving and always departing. My journey has taught me many things. Most important has been to continually be aware of how my way of knowing is shaped by the discursive production of power/ knowledge—and to resist, when I want to. Sometimes, I just love wallowing in certain pleasurable constructions of my self. But anyway, to get back to 'who' I have been in each of the countries I have lived in—in the USA, I have been an international graduate student. I am an untenured professor. I will always be a nomad in this country and I now desire multiple departings (and continued arrivings) in different spaces.

I am not a grand theorist or a major player in the field and this book is not a comprehensive presentation of theories about space or knowing. However, it does reflect a historical moment in the field. I recently asked a senior colleague what I should add to this text regarding epistemology. Her reply was "Everything is about epistemology!". The contribution I make here is to strategically use the work of a specific group of scholars who theorize about knowing and translate that theorizing into a vulgar theory that reflects curriculum studies issues and educational research awareness. The greatest compliment I have received on my previous work was when an external reviewer highlighted the usefulness of my explication of postmodern theories of knowing and the importance of the connections I made with practice. This book presents 'real' studies that reflect the use of complicated theory and brings together a specific research theory that highlights the need for in-depth data analysis and the study of the discursive production of *how we know what we know*.

And finally, the cover of the book highlights another issue. My academic self may comfortably theorize about home and journey but my heart resides in one geographic space at all times. That space is with my parents, looking out from their verandah over the Indian Ocean, to the most beautiful sunsets in the world. I took the photograph when I was home in 2005 and wanted to share it and memorialize it in my first major work. Thank you.

1
Curriculum Spaces Research Theory

This introductory chapter presents a discussion of the state of the field of Curriculum Studies and educational research. The discussion then moves into the current theorizing of an epistemological crisis that draws upon poststructural, postcolonial and psychoanalytic theories to lead us beyond static understandings of how we know to more fluid and complicated knowledge that reveals exclusions and objectifications at work in educational settings. The 'crisis' is a useful turn that is analyzed through the development of this avant-garde curriculum research theory called Curriculum Spaces. It is time "to produce different knowledge, to produce knowledge differently as we work for social justice in the human sciences" (St. Pierre, 2000, p. 27). This is a move for more accessible theorizing in Curriculum Studies as an ethical responsibility in these historically inscribed times.

It is time to bring recent important moves in understanding curriculum theory and educational research together to create an avant-garde movement—Curriculum Spaces does just that. This work is a response to Pinar's (2004) call for a more complicated conversation that centers interdisciplinary intellectuality, erudition and self-reflexivity. Therefore, in this book you will find the development of a curriculum theory that centers knowing and spaces of knowing as a discursive production that shapes the educational experience on all levels. This centering of epistemological spaces impacts the lives of Others. This strategic use of language highlights that *the way we know what we know* is a curriculum issue—a curriculum space. It is an ethical turn toward responsibility in research and away from simply theoretical meanderings (St. Pierre, 2000). This book responds to the call for engagement with specific complex problems in curriculum that do not have generalizable solutions (St. Pierre, 2000). You will find here an in-depth discussion of the state of the field of educational research marking it as vital text in future educational research courses.

Providing exemplars that bring together research and curriculum theory will lead the way into a new historic conjunction thus providing an avant-garde use of theory. Central to this new approach is a detailed discussion of foundational ideas of educational research and epistemology in Curriculum Studies, and it presents the development of this intersection in a number of different recent state of the educational research studies that lead the reader through the theory and the research itself (Lather, 2001a). Educational research, as a field, will also benefit greatly from this discussion, because it is time to do more than merely position the researcher in qualitative research. Lather (2004) states that it is time for a "turn toward more concrete efforts to put theory to work" (p. 2). It is time to call upon educational researchers to work to understand that the way they know what they know also impacts the lives of those they study and/or teach. This is a discursive and recursive relationship (Foucault, 1977; Jagodzinski, 2002). It is an ethical turn that has emerged from the linguistic turn. It is a 'making sense' of difficult knowledge and reflects the crisis of representation (Marcus and Fischer, 1986).

Curriculum Spaces Research Theory is an approach to investigating epistemological spaces as discursive productions from a poststructural/ postmodern perspective. It draws upon the notion of discourse as an absent power that validates and legitimizes. "A discourse author-ises certain people to speak and correspondingly silences others, or at least makes their voices less authoritative. A discourse is therefore exclusionary" (Usher and Edwards, 1994, p. 90). It moves the field of Curriculum from studying the self and the desire to 'give voice' to others to a more complicated understanding of how we are all framed by these historical, social and cultural discourses that, in effect, produce the possibilities of being. However, this effect of power is not linear, nor deterministic. Curriculum Spaces draws upon the Foucauldian notion that power circulates and actively produces knowledge and ways of being. This approach studies the manifestation of relationships within the social network. Therefore, the theory and research presented in this book consider social relationships and 'how we know' individuals, reform movements and educational and social discourses, as vital undertaking. As such, it should be investigated to produce a complicated understanding of subjectivities, and thus, move us beyond deterministic, simplistic desires for voices and stories. Because:

> Power is manifested as relationships in a social network. It comes from below, induced in the body and produced in social transactions. Power, through knowledge, brings forth active 'subjects' who better 'understand' their own subjectivity yet who in this very process subject themselves to forms of power (Usher and Edwards, 1994, p. 89).

This is a call for the study of how we are normalized, how we are embedded within total institutions and how we engage in and negotiate the production of legitimate knowledge. This embeddedness excludes certain ways of being and erases the bodies of those students, teachers, parents, custodians and others who are considered deviant, or outside the norm: pregnant teens, drop-outs, children of color, gay and lesbian teachers and students, female juvenile offenders, charter schools and alien academics. It is important to reveal the discourses themselves and how this knowing impacts the lives and possibilities of being for those we' know.'

This may not be tied to a particular subject position, but may be a discussion of how the discourses frame a reform movement and thus make possible certain ways of being within the movement and make impossible positions of deviance. For example, the Professional Development School reform movement in teacher education was an attempt to masculinize an historically 'female space,' thus devaluing feminized ways of knowing and calling for a 'medical school' approach to training teachers. It was exclusion through discourses at work. Along the same lines, whiteness is embedded in certain multicultural education discourses even as we attempt to create inclusive education. Therefore, we continue to rely upon the dominant lens and in effect, continue Othering children of color (see chapters three and four). Thus, investigating how we 'know others' and how educational and social discourses frame the possibilities of being in society (within and without educational settings) is the project presented here.

> Discourses embody meaning and social relationships, they constitute both subjectivity and power relations... Thus discourses construct certain possibilities for thought. They order and combine words in particular ways and exclude or displace other combinations (Ball, 1990c, p. 17 as cited in Usher and Edwards, 1994, p. 90).

Basically, it's all about knowing others and how that 'getting to know' is informed by the subject position we assumed the other inhabits and knowing ourselves (research positionality that is more than a confession). It is most important that we understand how we know Others—those who are considered deviant, less than, abnormal and are excluded by the dominant society. Often this knowing of others is shaped by race, class, gender and sexuality discourses. It is also influenced by historical, social and cultural knowledges. So, this approach is an epistemological study of curriculum and suggests that, by studying how we know (the relationship between the knower and the known), we can do a better job of interrupting exclusionary practices (reform movements and mandated educational change) and even provide possibilities for resisting the consumption and reduction of the Others.

The Crisis of Representation

The aim is to understand or reveal how we 'know' others—not fall into the trap of believing we can fully know or represent others as this leads to consumption of the other and the reduction of individuals' lives and beliefs into edible bytes (hooks, 1992). The crisis of representation in the social sciences that occurred in the late 20th century highlights the dangers of assuming you can research others lives and thus fully know them. Historically, the Mead, Boaz, and Malinowski traditions posited that, if you spent a year on the island, or a year in the bush with a 'tribe,' you could observe all of the seasons and festivals and thus come to fully know your subjects (often native and/or colonial subjects). A great deal of historical ethnographic research was harmful to the subjects and has led to the mistaken belief that still dominates today—a whimsical and seductive notion—that presenting the voice of others and persistent engagement in the field will lead to a 'real' representation (Behar, 1995).

> A 'crisis' of representation in the social sciences opens the way for the disruption of universalist assumptions of teacher and student, citizenship and democracy that underpin the dominant discourses in teacher education. The foundational goals of the social sciences arose from the political and administrative agendas of the early twentieth century American society (Popkewitz, 1991).

Scholars in anthropology have been talking about the changing culture of thought for nearly two decades now. Geertz (1983) and Clifford (1988) drew attention to the epistemological assumptions that framed our understanding of representation and being. According to Geertz (1983), "something is happening to the way we think about the way we think" (p. 20). And Clifford (1988) highlighted the increasing difficulties of describing cultural diversity as inscribed in bounded and independent cultures.

> It is more than ever crucial for different peoples to form complex concrete images of one another, as well as of the relationships of knowledge and power that connect them; but no sovereign scientific method or ethical stance can guarantee the truth of such images. They are constituted—the critique of colonial modes of representation has shown at least this much—in specific historical relations of dominance and dialogue (Clifford, 1988, p. 23).

Complicating images of sociocultural knowledge through an increasing awareness of multiple ways of knowing and being, and reconceptualizing space and time, is one way in which educational research and the field of Curriculum Studies may benefit from this crisis in the social sciences and move beyond the hegemonic realist perspective. Apple and St. Maurice (1991) outline the scene as one of inheritance and impossible goals. They suggest that in educational research we have inherited structures formed by Progressive Era reforms and social engineering. What has grown out of these reforms are institutions and professions that aim to produce a stable social order, but with the notions of social harmony and civil justice as elusive goals. Thus, they call for the educators of the current historical moment of struggle with the ethical and moral problems in a world that is less 'safe' than the Progressive reformers experienced in their optimistic fervor. It is a call to action.

Epistemology

> The refiguration of social theory represents, or will if it continues, a sea of change in our notion not so much of what knowledge is but of what it is we want to know (Geertz, 1983, p. 34).

Lincoln (1998) suggests that we move beyond attempts to fully know and the desire to describe the world that emerged from the Enlightenment. She calls for a more complicated search for knowledge and understanding in the postmodern moment. She responds to the crisis of representation by revealing the way modernist knowledge projects and research were founded upon the assumption that cultures and individual human subjects could be represented objectively and be fully known through generalizable cultural descriptions. It is important to note that any move to authorial voice (such as this very text) is always already in danger of reinscribing the real and producing another knowledge project. This is not an innocent act. Therefore, I highlight Lincoln's vital call for revealing modernist knowledge projects, while at the same time acknowledging the impossibility of innocence in this project. Lather (1996) also addresses this issue, when she describes modernity as framed by the assumptions of the authentic, whole self with a desire for originary moments and salvation narratives. It is time to interrupt such assumptions (and our desires for simplicity in research) by drawing upon postmodern theories and using a research method that investigates the discourses that frame such efforts. This is counterhegemonic work. However, this is not an attack on modernity. The 'post' here is more reminiscent of interruptions and revelations rather than oppositional or a call for new regimes of truth. It is, rather, a move to reveal how things play out (how modernity works), and thus, I suggest a different way of researching and understanding curriculum.

> Direct opposition often serves to confirm what it seeks to put into question by agreeing to operate within circumscribed limits which leave the system intact....More dramatically, acts of violence against a regime may serve the regime in question, for example, by rallying support for the status quo, even to the point where a regime might solicit or even fabricate such violence (Bernasconi, 1993, p. 97).

From a feminist and postcolonial perspective, Visweswaran (1994) suggests that the historical moment is marked by the failure of research practice. According to Visweswaran (1994), this research practice failure is a part of the process of knowledge production and is a sign of an epistemological crisis. It is a call for new ways of attempting the project of knowledge production.

> The epistemology this implies cannot be reconciled with a notion of cumulative scientific progress, and the partiality at stake is stronger than the normal scientific dictates that we study problems piecemeal, that we must not overgeneralize, that the best picture is built up by an accretion of rigorous evidence. Cultures are not 'scientific' objects (assuming such things exist, even in the natural sciences). Culture, and our views of 'it,' are produced historically, and are actively contested. There is no whole picture that can be 'filled in,' since the perception and filling of a gap lead to the awareness of other gaps (Clifford, 1986, p. 18).

Traditional realist epistemological assumptions have failed to convey the multiplicities of knowing and being, of flux and chaotic time, within cultures. Serres with Latour (1995) use the creation of the 'big science' of the Enlightenment as responsible for the violent assertion of power within the dominant paradigm. As a youth, Serres resigned from scientific and military schools. He states: "I was formed intellectually by science's internal revolutions, and philosophically by the relationship—internal and external—between science and violence. The latter question has dominated everything up to this point—both my life and my studies" (Serres with Latour, 1995, p. 18). Traditionally, science prescribed a static and fixed subject which, according to Serres, spawned static systems of knowing and histories of being even though they claimed to describe a process of becoming. He states: "It's better to paint a sort of fluctuating picture of relations and rapports—like the percolating basin of a glacial river, unceasingly changing its bed and showing an admirable network of forks, some of which freeze or silt up, while others open up—or like a cloud of angels that passes, or the list of prepositions, or the dance of flames" (Serres with Latour, 1995, p. 105).

This epistemological transformation requires a 'state-of-flux' philosophy, such as described in the work of Michel Serres (1993). Destabilizing and disrupting essentialist assumptions provides possibilities for other ways of knowing. Bringing together time and 'networks of knowing' challenges researchers to develop an increased awareness of the fluctuation and bifurcation of cultural understanding.

As Clifford (1988, 1997), Marcus and Fischer (1986) and Geertz (1983) struggled with issues of cultural representation, so Serres and Latour (1995) struggle with rethinking the way we think about thinking. According to Serres and Latour, the traditional epistemological assumptions that framed scientific research perpetuated a sense of safety in distance and the creation of absolutes in cultural representations. It did not ask any questions on the relationship between science and violence, or science and imperialism, appropriation and colonialization. Serres with Latour (1995) stated that "everything was taking place as if the scientific Ivory Tower were inhabited by good children—naive, hardworking, and meticulous, of good conscience and devoid of any political or military horizons. But weren't they the contemporaries of the Manhattan Project, which prepared the bomb?" (Serres with Latour, 1995, p. 16).

Postmodern Theories

The Curriculum Spaces Research Theory draws upon poststructural, postcolonial and psychoanalytic theories of knowing. In each chapter you will find detailed theorizing as a result of the investigation contained in that chapter. Here, I intend to give a brief overview of the theories as I see them. This is not a comprehensive analysis of these fields of thought. Rather it is an attempt to make sense of the positions I take, so that you will find the exemplars more understandable. For example, the early work of Foucault (1977) used a genealogical approach to historicize the discourses that legitimized knowledge and led to individual subjects self-regulating through state apparatuses and through economies of power. These state apparatuses were total institutions, such as education, hospitals and military. This idea of the normalization of ways of being that emerged as a result of the effects of power are vital in this discussion of Curriculum Spaces.

Poststructuralism and Foucault. Foucault was a French poststructuralist who worked to reveal the regimes of truth and the technologies of power that shape and are shaped by the subject/object relationships in discursive relationships (Popkewitz and Brennan, 1998). Foucault (1977) directly challenges the notion that schools (or universities) can naturally or neutrally 'create' empowered and emancipated citizens. According to Foucault, regimes of truth that regulate and reinscribe the power relations of the institutions are discourses that function as a dominant 'Truth' and thus regulate the behavior and ideological assumptions of the institution:

> Each society has its régime of truth, its 'general politics' of truth: that is, the types of discourse which it accepts and makes function as true; the mechanisms and instances which enable one to distinguish true and false statements, the means by which each is sanctioned; the techniques and procedures accorded value in the acquisition of truth; the status of those who are charged with saying what counts as true (Foucault, 1980, p. 131).

Foucault (1977) described how the disciplinary practices upon the bodies of the students, patients and troops were violent and coercive as they produced docile bodies and obedient souls. This is applicable to contemporary settings because we continue to categorize, measure, normalize and regulate children in schools. It creates governable students—"In disciplining the body, persons as subjects become governable, thus marginalizing the need for coercion in the regulation of populations" (Foucault, 1977, p. 92). However, the human subject is an active knowing subject and the resulting epistemological space is one shaped by the effects of power, but also negotiated and multiply positioned. The child/student/individual is knowing, but is also acted upon through surveillance and the use of authority as effects of power. This leads to self-regulation shaped by the technologies of power (for example, standardized testing) and legitimate discourses. It is vital to note that this subjugation also produces the possibility of resistance and this is often lost in discussions of Foucault's work. This suggests a less deterministic approach—that epistemological spaces are negotiated and power is fluid. Of course, we continue to be framed by the metanarratives of humanism, and social and educational discourses, but by revealing how these discourses play out—how they work—we can interrupt them.

Foucault's work presents stories of power and the ways it changes—knowledge and power are contingent. He interrupts the 'story of progress' and suggests that even attempts at emancipation and liberation are embedded within modernist discourses (Usher and Edwards, 1994). Therefore, humanism does not remove power—it merely reinscribes it—uses it differently. As a result, "We are no more 'human', 'emancipated', or 'rational' now compared to our historical predecessors, simply different (Marshall, 1990, p. 21)" (cited in Usher and Edwards, 1994, p. 84).

One way to sustain rigorous questioning of the truth embodied in educational work and research is to articulate and disrupt the 'natural' (neutral) foundations of the dominant discourses (Popkewitz and Brennan, 1998). Truth, according to Foucault, is played out in the three-dimensional space of knowledge, subjectivity and power (Simola, Heikkinen, and Silvonen, 1998). This suggests that an investigation of the production of 'truth' and the 'subject' might reveal the ways in which the educational institutions have excluded and silenced marginal discourses.

Psychoanalytic Theory and Freud. The psychoanalytic theory used here is based upon Pitt (1998) and Britzman's (1998, 2003) use of Freud's notion of the unconscious—the unconscious in education. It enables us to consider issues of modernist desires and the impossibility of 'arriving' so that we consistently interrupt our own research attempts to fully know or assume knowledge about subject positions. We can then add to the picture of epistemological spaces as Curriculum Spaces by including the analysis of discourses of the self.

> The problem is that psychoanalytic theories complicate all our stories of engagement with knowledge by insisting upon the role of unconscious processes in the making of such stories. These complications reside within knowledge itself, and they circulate in the stories told to us, in our retellings of them as research stories, and in our readings of such retellings (Pitt, 1998, p. 536).

Freud, as outlined by Pitt (1998), believed that the unconscious is a destination that we can never reach. Therefore, our understanding of this is deferred and delayed because it is complicated, fluid, and messy and we cannot know. "One never arrives because the unconscious is dynamic, forever creating itself anew from the bits and pieces of everyday life that remind us of wishes that are taboo and experiences that are too painful to confront head on" (Pitt, 1998, p. 541).

Britzman (1998) turns our attention to the foundations/possibilities of education to deconstruct education, pedagogy and learning. Britzman presents the dream of education as an object of desire of 'school men.' In this way, she is able to reveal how the foundational concepts of education emerged as change, progress, betterment and advancement. This takes the focus on epistemological spaces from the individual to the societal. These concepts are tied to arguments over social engineering, nation building and economics, and the institutionalization of education/schooling. So, Britzman (1998) suggests that education wishes to be deliberate (conscious) by building the 'big' stage of education on the 'little' stage of individual development. The unconscious of education must be buried:

> But the repressed returns in the form of symptoms. Unsatisfied, yet still in dialogue with the official stories of the schoolmen from Horace Mann to John Dewey, and with the popular news accounts of various moral panics between 1830–1914 that imagined the working class, the foreigners, and the rural populations as in need of containment, order, and Christian morality (Britzman, 1998, p. 54).

Britzman (1998) outlines how pedagogy (and we might add here, curriculum) has emerged as the new object of incitement in the field of education and the fields of the humanities and social sciences—all of which are preoccupied with the promises and dangers of pedagogy. This reveals Curriculum Spaces as the constructions upon the little stage of education of the 'proper' way of being—the normalized self—the possible. And it leads to conflict—and resistance, repressed in the form of symptoms (e.g., dropouts, school violence and teen pregnancies).

> When all of these fields are considered most generally, when education *writ large* questions its relation to social justice with the suggestion that education can be made from the proper teacher, the proper curriculum, or the proper pedagogy so that learning will be no problem to the actors involved, we might note that for there to be a learning there must be conflict within learning (Britzman, 1998, p. 5).

This enables us to complicate our understanding of discourses and epistemologies as objects of desire at the societal, institutional and individual levels. It also creates a position that highlights the impossibility of arriving and the unknowable and inconsolability of Curriculum Spaces (Britzman, 1998).

Postcolonial Theories. Postcolonial theories of knowing were also used to understand how we know and how we live. Clifford (1988, 1992, 1997), Kaplan (1996), Gilroy (1993), Pratt (1992), Dubois (1995), and Bhabha (1994) use a variety of terms to discuss the movement of cultures and the global and local forces that shape them and enhance the kinesthetic quality of culture. "'Cultures' do not hold still for their portraits—they are dynamic. Attempts to make them do so always involve simplification and exclusion, selection of a temporal focus, the construction of a partial self-other relationship, and the imposition or negotiation of a power relationship" (Clifford, 1986, p. 10).

> It does so through a postmodern vision of seemingly improbable juxtapositions, the global collapsed into and made an integral part of parallel, related local situations, rather than being something monolithic and external to them. This move toward comparison as juxtaposition firmly deterritorializes culture in ethnographic writing. It also stimulates accounts of cultures composed in a landscape for which there is as yet no developed theoretical conception (Marcus, 1994, p. 566).

For example, Clifford (1997) challenges postmodern ethnographic representations to enhance the cultural performance of space and place. This is a counterhegemonic discourse that extends cultural boundaries and highlights the "transgressive intercultural frontiers of nations, peoples, and locales. Stasis and purity are asserted—against historical forces of movement and contamination" (Clifford, 1997, p. 7). This requires a blurring of modernistic boundaries. Clifford (1997) thus calls for an inherently partial analysis that makes it possible to work against the essentialist traditions of ethnography and modernist research, in general. However, Clifford believes every focus excludes and no methodology or terminology is innocent. "It follows that there is no cure for the troubles of cultural politics in some old or new vision of consensus or universal values. There is only more translation" (Clifford, 1997, p. 13).

However, Visweswaran (1994) approaches this from another perspective. She demands a feminist critique within the postcolonial moment that highlights issues of deterritorialization and global homelessness. She situates the practices of First World anthropologists as privileged and colonizing in their knowledge production and as a masculine way of knowing that eradicates the home as a site of theory. And Bhabha (1994) presents the possibility of going 'beyond' establishing epistemological boundaries, to consider:

> a bridge, where 'presencing' begins because it captures something of the estranging sense of the relocation of the home and the world—the unhomeliness—that is the condition of extra-territorial and cross-cultural initiations. To be unhomed is not to be homeless, nor can the 'unhomely' be easily accommodated in that familiar division of social life into private and public spheres (Bhabha, 1994, p. 9).

Bhabha (1994) and Ong (1995) highlight the home (local, indigenous, individual) as a site for feminist resistance against the patriarchal and gendered nature of social reality by interrogating the domestic space as normalizing and the personal/public binary as regulatory. Both scholars use this concept of the unhomed to create a space for cultural difference. "The unhomely moment relates to the traumatic ambivalences of a personal, psychic history to the wider disjunctions of political existence" (Bhabha, 1994, p. 11).

> Private and public, past and present, the psyche and the social develop an interstitial intimacy. It is an intimacy that questions binary divisions through which such spheres of social experience are often spatially opposed. These spheres of life are linked through an 'in-between' temporality that

takes the measure of dwelling at home, while producing an image of the world of history (Bhabha, 1994, p. 13).

This move in postcolonial thought is useful in the ways it historicizes First World knowledge production on the bodies of the colonized and calls for a more feminized, complicated understanding of the construction of epistemological spaces. Spivak (1993) calls this "search of the differentially contaminated face of the absolutely other" (p. 177). She also positions Western feminist research (and knowledge production) as not innocent, and highlights the impossibility of a mere translation of the voice of Others:

> There is nothing necessarily meretricious about the Western feminist gaze.... On the other hand, there is nothing essentially noble about the lay of the majority either. It is merely the easiest way of being 'democratic' with minorities. In the act of wholesale translation into English there can be a betrayal of the democratic ideal into the law of the strongest (Spivak, 1993, p, 182).

Using postcolonial work in this way is a call for a " new politics of reading," that Spivak (1993) outlines as moving beyond excuses and accusations to establish critical intimacy. She reminds us that we cannot fight imperialism by perpetuating a new 'orientalism,' a new Othering. We are all embedded within the historical colonial project, even within the United States of America. We are not outside the postcolonial globe. However, we are always already in danger of our desire as researchers for a homogenous group, an originary group that can be formed (or known and consumed) as an ethnocultural concrete collective. This is an inscribed space, according to Spivak, and is the result of a dominant technology of power. Our work is not outside of such effects of power, and it is not innocent.

> Our inclination to obliterate the difference between United States internal colonization and the dynamics of the decolonized space makes use of this already established ethnocultural agenda. At worst it secures the 'they' of development and aggression against the constitutional 'we'. At best, it suits our institutional convenience and brings the rest of the world home. A certain double standard, a certain sanctioned ignorance, can now begin to operate in the areas of the study of central and so-called marginal cultures (Spivak, 1993, p. 279).

Therefore, we must persistently critique the discursive structures we inhabit and our ways of being as researchers and researched and reveal the desires and myths that shape us. Spivak (1993) demands that we understand how we cannot NOT want to inhabit societal myths, discourses and other effects of power because we are embedded within them. This is a move to complicate her notion of strategic essentialism while still centering the epistemic violence of colonialism. "The clearest available example of such epistemic violence is the remotely orchestrated, far-flung, and heterogeneous project to constitute the colonial subject as Other" (Spivak, 1995, p. 25). This subaltern position (Othering) is produced through subjugated knowledge and normative narratives. Curriculum Spaces Research Theory calls for an awareness of the way this plays out in education.

> When we come to the concommittant question of the consciousness of the subaltern, the notion of what the work *cannot* say becomes important.... 'The subject' implied by the texts of insurgency can only serve as a counterpossibility for the narrative sanctions granted to the colonial subject in the dominant groups. The postcolonial intellectuals learn that their privilege is their loss. In this they are a paradigm of intellectuals (Spivak, 1995, p. 28).

As a result, Spivak (1995) suggests the epistemic violence of imperialism provides an imperfect allegory of the way violence is part of the possibility (the production) of epistemological spaces. It is vital that we consider violence and coercion as effects of power in the production of Curriculum Spaces. Parry (1995) refers to Spivak's work when she says:

> Where military conquest, institutional compulsion and ideological interpellation was, epistemic violence and devious discursive negotiations requiring of the native that he rewrite his position as object of imperialism, is; and in place of recalcitrance and refusal enacted in movements of resistance and articulated in oppositional discourses, a tale is told of the self-consolidating other and the disarticulated subaltern (p. 38).

Parry (1995) also uses the work of Bhabha as a call for the scrutiny of discursive systems as instances of transgression performed by the Other (native) within and against colonial discourses—again highlighting resistance and refusal in epistemological spaces.

Therefore, the move presented here is multidimensional. It is the study of discourse practices that utilizes a poststructural perspective, a psychoanalytic perspective and a postcolonial perspective to shift the focus away from the critical realist interpretation to a more complicated study of the formation of the subject/culture by looking at the way we live out our lives in this contested terrain of contradictory positions and symbolic exchanges (Lather, 1996).

> Critical appropriations of postmodernism focus on the regulatory and transgressive functions of discourses that articulate and organize our everyday experiences of the world. To both confirm and complicate received codes is to see how language is inextricably bound to the social and the ideological. This moves social inquiry to new grounds, the grounds of 'discourse,' where the ways we talk and write are situated within social practices, the historical conditions of meaning, the positions from which texts are both produced and received (Lather, 1996, p. 360).

Critical Discourse Analysis

Therefore, this work falls under the deconstructivist paradigm with critical overtones. What does that mean? Well, as outlined above, the position of the theory is that we cannot fully represent others—rather we should work to complicate our understanding of their subject positions and how these subject positions are created (and refused). This has elements of social construction of knowledge, which suggests a critical or constructivist paradigm. However, the interest of this move toward epistemological spaces, or curriculum spaces, focuses on the subject. It is important to note here that discussions of epistemology often blur the boundaries between knowing and being—thus including elements of ontology in the discussion. Ontology is concerned with 'what is' (Crotty, 1998, p. 10). So, in the discussion of 'ways' of being, or how we know what we know as subject/object, I am also drawing upon ontological issues (Foucault, 1977). Therefore, any discussion of being suggests ontological considerations. Crotty (1998) states that ontological issues and epistemological issues often arise together. For the sake of clarification, however, I want to highlight that the Curriculum Spaces approach centers the focus on epistemological issues—the study of *ways* of being (not the nature of being which leans more toward an ontological focus) and how we know what we know—specifically, how we know Others (Crotty, 1998). It is a research theory designed to reveal the meaning-making processes in educational research and reveal research positionality as an act of knowing. What remains unclear in the debate within critical pedagogy is the relationship (or tension) between utopian thought, values, and pragmatic theory. In other words, while the postmodern and poststructuralist critique has led many radical educators to accept the problematic and contingent nature of all values—including those of radical democracy—there remains an inclination on the part of critical educators to employ such contingent values (e.g., agency, emancipation, freedom, empowerment, democracy, justice, solidarity, etc.) as the basis of a utopian view to orient sociocultural formation (Stanley, 1992, p. 172).

> Subjectivity is often considered the epistemological theory of all qualitative research. However, in this instance, it is more about how subject positions are framed and thus 'known'—not how the individual researcher situates themselves in the research project (positionality). So, as we move into the realm of subjectivities, and the relationship between the knower and the known, we must move beyond a deterministic humanist position to a different definition of power, agency, and desire (Lather, 1996).

Studying the discursive practices surrounding the epistemological spaces at the multiple levels of knowing enables us to understand the effects of power underlying the space: "A discursive structure can be detected because of the systematicity of the ideas, opinions, concepts, ways of thinking and behaving which are formed within a particular context, and because of the effects of those ways of thinking and behaving" (Mills, 1997, p. 17). In this book you will find chapters that focus on one or more of the 'levels'—however, this is not to suggest that meaning-making occurs in a linear or demarcated fashion on each level. The discursive production of subjectivity is both and an ongoing project on multiple levels at all times. The chapters that focus on one specific level, such as chapter three looking at societal constructions or chapter five highlighting the local or personal level, are utilized to reveal the way some studies look at particular levels but at all times it should be understood that the multiple levels of knowing blur and blend in a messy way within and against the discursive production or legitimization of the subject.

Mills (1997) discusses how the legitimization of knowledge and 'truth' emerges from a position of dominance when she says, "Colonial power enables the production of knowledge, and it also maps out powerful positions from which to speak" (p. 115). This enables us to conceptualize power as discursive and fluid, using the work of Foucault (1977) and Serres with Latour (1995). Thus, we may produce a 'text' that highlights the messy and dangerous construction of subject through the discourses that shape our interpretation of text (Mills, 1997).

> The notion of discourse is ambiguous in Foucault. A thinking of discourse as *both* what is said and what is done, which breaks down the distinction between language (discourse in the narrow sense) and practice, is much closer to what I think he intends than just language, but this is not always how he uses the term himself. Unfortunately, most people who use the word discourse think he is talking about what people say. For me, the only function of discourse is to end the action/language distinction (Stuart Hall as quoted in Osborne and Segal, 1999, p. 398).

The other issue that is raised and addressed in this book is the idea that the field requires not only theories for understanding—but also guidelines and exemplars for research, and complicating researcher positionality. The innovative aspect is to present the theories in the first chapters and then provide exemplars of the research method. Thus, I outline and demonstrate how the method of Critical Discourse Analysis (Fairclough, 1995) can be used in studying Curriculum Spaces. This is a three-level model of analysis of discourses and moves through the social, institutional and local levels of discourse. This is extremely useful for this book as it allows the study of discourses at multiple levels and thus adds to the understanding of how individual ways of being are made possible (and impossible, or deviant) on a multiplicity of levels. So, this takes us from the individual, or local level, to the ways institutions are an effect of power, to the social and educational discourses that frame our lives. The method of Critical Discourse Analysis, outlined by Fairclough (1995), suggests that the analysis of spoken and written language texts as discourse practices (text production, distribution and consumption) reveals how the discursive events are instances of socio-cultural practice. It enables the broad conceptualization of 'text':

> A rather broader conception has become common within discourse analysis, where a text may be either written or spoken discourse, so that, for example, the words used in a conversation (or their written transcription) constitute a text. In cultural analysis, by contrast, texts do not need to be linguistic at all; any cultural artefact—a picture, a building, a piece of music—can be seen as a text (Fairclough, 1995, p. 4).

Analyzing texts in this way provides insights into what is and what is not included, what is taken as given (common sense). It is one way of analyzing the ideological content (underpinning assumptions) of texts. Thus, texts are studied as social spaces and are interrogated simultaneously as spaces of cognition and representation of the world and social interaction. "This multifunctionality of language in texts can be used to operationalize theoretical claims about the socially constitutive properties of discourse and text (Foucault, 1972, quoted in Fairclough, 1995, p. 6). The texts studied in this book include: the educational reform movement in teacher education, known as the Professional Development School; the historical constructions of female juvenile offenders; Charter Schools; films about teachers; and, my positionality as an Alien academic in a post-9/11 world.

Why? Because studying "discourse practice ensures attention to the historicity of discursive events by showing both their continuity with the past (their dependence upon given orders of discourse) and their involvement in making history (their remaking of orders of discourse)" (Fairclough, 1995, p. 11). Therefore, Critical Discourse Analysis is a method of social research that focuses on textual analysis, intertextual analysis, and sociocultural considerations to reveal the ways in which social relations of power (and epistemological spaces) are produced, distributed and consumed. Using interviews, observation, documents and any other form of data as a text, requires a three level analysis. According to Gavey (1997), these three levels are:

- Description of the text;
- Interpretation of discourse practice/s; and,
- Explanation of the situational, institutional and societal texts.

In the exemplars of research presented in this book you will find the results of this three-level analysis.

> I see discourse as a complex of three elements: social practice, discoursal practice (text production, distribution and consumption), and text, and the analysis of a specific discourse calls for analysis in each of these dimensions and their interrelations. The hypothesis is that significant connections exist between features of texts, ways in which texts are put together and interpreted, and the nature of the social practice (Fairclough, 1995, p. 74).

Ultimately, this method enables a move from contextual discussions about reform in teacher education and experiential anecdotes, for example, to more complicated discussions of the epistemological assumptions framing Curriculum Spaces. However, Fairclough (1995) calls for vigilance about the use of the results of this method and demands that we critique the outcome as in danger of helping to further naturalize (neutralize and consume) different ideological practices.

The methodological practice of cultural representation is no longer inviolable. The totalizing assumptions that shaped educational research (and, historically ethnography) as constructing impartial, objective accounts of static cultures and fascinating Others is under assault. Critiques of traditional research practices have highlighted the limits of representation and the historical implications for its role in colonial oppression (Visweswaran, 1994; Marcus and Fischer, 1986). Issues of subjectivity, gendered silences, representational partiality, and the implications of the colonizing mentality, to name a few, have been highlighted by a number of authors, according to Van Maanen (1995). Bringing together the postmodern theories and the study of discourse methods discussed above has created a new way of looking at curriculum and of doing educational research. I outline the rationale behind the development of this analytical method in the next chapter.

Conclusion

> In contemporary school reforms, these foundational assumptions are deeply embedded as doxa. Dominant and liberal educational reform discourses tend to instrumentally organize change as logical and sequential, although there has been some recognition of the pragmatic qualities of social life (see, e.g., Fullan with Stiegelbauer, 1991). Although the specific focus may change, the agents of redemption are the State and educational researchers, and the agents of change are teachers as 'self'-motivated professionals (Popkewitz and Brennan, 1998, p. 7).

It is all about peeling back the layers of discourse that frame our lives and the lives of others. This is made possible by the study of individual subject positions, how discourses play out in educational institutions, reform movements and social and educational discourses. Like an onion, if we peel back the layers we can then gain a more adequate understanding and thus negotiate the effects of power. Then we might be able to create spaces of emancipation and equity that address the contingent forms of knowledge and power in which we are all embedded.

We can use Curriculum Spaces Research Theory in a variety of ways. For example: to study the ways our own lives are shaped, how we know and how we know Others (especially as the 'researched'); to investigate social constructions of deviance and exclusion (especially through raced, gendered, classes and sexualized knowings); to study the institutional effects of power (e.g., school buildings, classrooms, teachers, custodial staff, students, parents and administrators), reform movements and mandated educational changes, and social and educational discourses.

We can then look for how the following knowings play out in our lives as researchers and educators. For example, the epistemic violence of our desires, the colonizing tendencies of power, social constructions of the subject, the normalization projects of regimes of truth, self-regulation, resistances and refusals, the interruptions of the unconscious, messy and fluid spaces of knowing and more. Who we are and how we know is the focus of this book. It is more than naval gazing and less than therapy. Curriculum Spaces Research Theory is all about revealing spaces of knowing/being. The idea is to draw our attention to the study of curriculum, and education in general, to the way individuals are restricted to certain 'normal' ways of being. These normalities include notions of the good girl, the successful student, and the manly man. However, we do not all fall, or want to fall, into such complete positions of obedience. And some of us are not given the chance to conform for our bodies, our ways of being, are considered deviant and abnormal. So, I suggest that by understanding how these constructions of exclusion work, we can move beyond research that reproduces essentialist understandings of the 'voices' of the oppressed, to reveal possibilities for resistance and interruption by individuals. Therefore, by knowing more about how children, students, girls, boys, teachers, parents and administrators are coerced and reduced to certain 'acceptable' socially constructed spaces of being, we can work to interrupt such constructions.

2
The Methodological Journey

You now have a picture of the theoretical lenses I utilized in Curriculum Spaces Research Theory. The necessity for the development of this vulgar theory emerged as a result of a dissatisfaction with research methodology and data analysis. Very early on I felt that the qualitative methodologies I encountered when doing educational research were more about validating methods of data collection than providing any ideas about data analysis. Over the last few years, when advising doctoral students in their dissertation research, I have also wondered about this failure of methodology—a failure to analyze beyond simplistic coding and themes. There seems to exist a lack of analysis in a vacuum of methodology. Quite often I have found in educational research of all types, a disconnect between the set up—the literature review or theoretical frame—and the analysis. As a result, the conclusions or findings are separate from and uninformed by the theoretical frame. Therefore, although I hesitated to announce my Curriculum Spaces work to be a 'research theory,' I decided to go ahead as a call for increased attention to analysis in educational research.

In order to arrive at the moment of a coalesced research theory, I have traveled through a number of different qualitative methodologies. In this chapter I will present a selection of my earlier efforts in educational research. As you read through it you will find the streams of thought and directionality that led to the development of this theory. As painful as it is to revisit earlier work, it is also a vital exercise. By revealing this journey, I intend to illustrate choices and the merging of theory and practice for novice educational researchers. From the very beginning of my research career, during my master's program in Canada, I had questions that led me beyond the immediate methodological tool. In the first section of this chapter I revisit that life history research project. Secondly, I outline some of the rather unusual redefinition efforts in my dissertation work that led to the beginning of theorizing discourse, travel and space in research. At that time it was still presented 'within' a methodology. And finally, I discuss my dissatisfaction with Critical and Deconstructivist research in what I call a failure of positionality. This chapter ends, therefore, with a call for the study of discourse and epistemological spaces in educational research. Thus, we can move beyond methodology to data analysis in the research exemplars in the next few chapters.

Life History—Revisiting Irene

My first methodological publication was a cry for help (Cary, 1999a). I was very disturbed by the failure of the life history methodology to prepare me for the stories I would hear. I actually began by critiquing the patriarch of the methodology, Ivor Goodson (1998). He had written of his concerns with the use and misuse of life history as a research method in recent times however, he seemed to employ a rather authoritative and patriarchal standpoint, from my point of view, as he outlined a number of concerns he perceived were arising from simplistic efforts presenting decontextualized life stories that served to romanticize and idealize the 'voices' of the research participants. He highlighted some important issues and I agreed that it was definitely time to problematize this desire for totalizing essentialist stories that often emerge 'in the name of' life history research. What was extremely useful to me was that Goodson's essay was another attempt to bring postmodern moment to bear on 'situating knowledge' through life history. However, I was disappointed. It was yet another failure, another avoidance of the necessary fictions of the method inscribed by the redemptive project of the social and human sciences (Popkewitz, 1998c). It seemed that Goodson (1998) believed he could fix the problem by highlighting the need for triangulation of data collection as a methodological validity tool that would overcome the shortfalls of decontextualized life stories. According to Goodson (1998), employing a critical analysis of life history through a study of the sociohistorical context would alleviate many of the issues with this method. At the time I was sure it was much more complicated than that, but it took me another couple of years of working through my concerns and issues as I went onto my doctoral studies in the United States before I could come up with some possible answers.

Why? Because in my novice educational research project for my master's degree in Canada, my own work using Life History methodology failed to contextualize the stories of my participants sufficiently and, as a result, I was uncomfortable with the data. The move I made was to stand in a different position. I had been comfortable with a Critical approach to the project. However, this method was more complex and less easily validated than mere attendance to methodological concerns. My questions revolved around the issue of knowing. What were the epistemological assumptions framing this method? How was it historicized within the culture of the modernist knowledge project (Lincoln, 1998)? In the discussion that emerged from this life history project I aimed to complicate the assumptions that frame this genre by highlighting the epistemological underpinnings and by historicizing the method within the larger modernist project. This highlights the modernist failures or authorizing fictions (Visweswaran, 1994) of Life History method as one way to problematize and complicate what is in danger of becoming a victory narrative within the redemptive culture of the social sciences.

Goodson (1998) searched for originary moments and as he also highlights a call for the "authentic Self" in his work on life history. Goodson goes on to present life history as a momentary glimpse into the life story of the research participant, yet in doing so he created an epistemological turn toward a realist ontology when he states that by contextualizing it we can establish more 'truth.' He continues: "To establish a broader picture we need to locate the stories and collaborate in the discussion and understanding of stories and narratives. A life, it is assumed, is cut of whole cloth, and its many pieces, with careful scrutiny, can be fitted into proper place. But this writing of a life...is constantly being created as it is written" (Goodson, 1998, p. 10). His work continues to be singular, selective and specific yet he failed to problematize that framing of knowledge and identity. He called for an increased awareness of multiple selves in multiple locations yet fails to blur location and time. He makes location static and idealizes collaboration. He reinscribed a romantic voice while attempting to move beyond the personal to the professional:

> The focus on the personal and practical teachers' stories is then an abdication of the right to speak on matters of social and political construction. By speaking in this voice about personal and practical matters the teacher loses a voice in the moment of speaking, for the voice that has been encouraged and granted, in the realm of personal and practical stories, is the voice of technical competency, the voice of the isolated classroom practitioner. The voice of 'ours not to reason why, ours but to do or die' (Goodson, 1998, p. 13).

Thus, contextualizing life history as a methodology suggested a 'validity' superior to a more situated consideration of ethics. According to Smith (1993), methodology in positivist paradigms established validity and solved the criteria problem. However, "just as the traditional empiricist theory of knowledge can no longer offer a coherent account of how to distinguish knowledge from opinion, methodology can no longer stand as the referent point from resolving the practice-level issue of distinguishing good from bad research" (Smith, 1993, p. 9). Thus, I decided it was time to rethink the assumptions that framed this research method.

In 1995, Hatch and Wisniewski edited *Life History and Narrative*, a collection of essays raising issues and questions surrounding related research methodologies under the umbrella terms 'Life History and Narrative.' Topics ranged from attempts to define the methodologies, terms and validities within these areas of research to discussions of the tensions arising from issues of 'voice' and collaboration. In most cases the essays continued to idealize 'voice' (multiple voices, teachers' voices, marginalized voices) as the central contribution of such methodologies. However, very little attention was paid to the ways in which life history and narrative methodologies were historically situated. As I discussed in chapter one, the crisis of representation in the social sciences (Marcus and Fischer, 1986) was central to this discussion:

> The task, particularly now, is not to escape the deeply suspicious and critical nature of the ironic mode of writing, but to embrace and utilize it in combination with other strategies for producing realist descriptions of society. The desirability of reconciling the persistence of irony with other modes of representation derives in turn from a recognition that because all perspectives and interpretations are subject to critical review, they must finally be left as multiple and open-ended alternatives. The only way to an accurate view and confident knowledge of the world is through a sophisticated epistemology that takes full account of intractable contradiction, paradox, irony, and uncertainty in the explanation of human activities. This seems to be the spirit of the developing responses across disciplines to what we described as a contemporary crisis of representation (Marcus and Fischer, 1986, p. 15).

This crisis moved the methodology of ethnography toward an increased political and historical awareness. This in turn redefined the conceptualization of cultural diversity. In terms of life history as a method, this crisis moved the study of research participants' lived experience to the center of the production of knowledge in the social sciences. Polkinghorne (1995) states that "a storied narrative is the linguistic form that preserves the complexity of human action with its interrelationship of temporal sequence, human motivation, chance happenings, and changing interpersonal and environmental contexts" (p. 7). A factual base is called for in much of the literature on Life History research as "without a factual base, narrative inquiry would run the danger of wild speculation" (Blumenfeld-Jones, 1995, p. 27). Therefore, a constant theme is the reaffirmation of realist assumptions within the genre and the need for rigor through contextualization and collaboration. Goodson (1995, 1998) and Barone (1995) extended this discussion by focusing on the power relations of life history research. Not fully trusting the story accounts as 'truthful' is one issue discussed in Barone's (1995) essay and he presents a solution with the concept of *emancipatory educational storysharing* as one way of working within and against the limits of this research method.

By bringing to bear this postmodern turn on life history research means the author (and the storyteller) may no longer claim universal truth or the neutral translation of reality. This provides a very useful point of departure for a more situated life history as tied to issues of meaning-making, history and power (Barone, 1995). However, Barone continued to present a victory narrative through the use of humanist notions of emancipation and agency. For example, "the rewards of emancipatory educational storysharing—singular, liberating moments of heightened awareness in which new definition is given to the selves of others and to one's own being—are worth the effort" (Barone, 1995, p. 73) Barone's (1995) work was powerful and provided a place from which to trouble the humanist foundations of life history methodology and thus I found this very useful and asserted that the possibilities of life history as a methodology and postpositivist research in general may be extended (Cary, 1999a). I suggested that using a poststructuralist feminist perspective through the concept of 'fiction' as described by Visweswaran (1994) would address this issue. Visweswaran highlighted the way the authorizing fictions of ethnography reinscribed authorial and essentialist representations of Others and she historicized the connection between ethnography and autobiography:

> Autobiographies are, of course, fictions of the self, but in my view, this emphasis on pluralism leads to a notion of 'trying on identities,' which obscures the fact that identities, no matter how strategically deployed, are

not always chosen, but are in fact constituted by relations of power always historically determined (Visweswaran, 1994, p. 8).

In the same way authorial fictions have now come into question, researchers also become fictions as our participants (or subjects) write or speak back through stories that we then attempt to re-present as 'truth.' The myths and authorizing fictions that frame life history must be interrogated as the best contemporary myth, according to Serres, that science is purged of all myths (Serres with Latour, 1995). The very label for this research is a myth. How can we 're-present' another's life history? There is much that remains hidden. What is shared and why? Life history projects are a mediated space that require a sociocultural construction of an individual's life/identity. Although much of the research around life history has focused on issues of representation, voice and context (Hatch and Wisniewski, 1995), ultimately it has failed to highlight the myths of such issues. Problematizing the issues listed above does not absolve the researcher from responsibility. Assumptions include: It is possible to re-present an individual's life history; life history method allows the research participant's voice to be heard; a life history is a concrete and neutral yet subjectively mediated event; there are no unrelated or unexpected stories in life history research. Visweswaran (1994) states:

> *Fictions of Feminist Ethnography* clearly calls attention to its own textuality, but it does so in order to better understand the politics of representation, how different narrative strategies may be authorized at specific moments in history by complex negotiations of community, identity. And accountability. Fiction, as we know, is political (p. 15).

This discussion was made possible by the emergence of an unexpected life history that arose from my research in 1995. What do you do with unexpected stories? Stories of resistance? Unrelated stories? How may the notion of authorizing fictions enable such re-presentations to inform the field in general? Much of what erupts in life history research remains hidden in the realist tales used to re-present the data:

> We should invent a theory of obscure, confused, dark, nonevident knowledge—a theory of 'adelo-knowledge.' This lovely adjective, with feminine resonances, means something that is hidden and does not reveal itself. The Greek island of Delos was once called Adelos, the hidden one. If you have tried to approach it, you surely know that it is usually hidden in

clouds and fog. Shadow accompanies light just as antimatter accompanies matter (Serres with Latour, 1995, p. 148).

I realized at this time the field of educational research needed to move beyond a desire for realist representations to a place of interrogation of the fictions that frame the search for 'truth' within victory narratives of the redemptive culture of the social sciences (Popkewitz, 1998c). And in order to re-frame 'truth,' we must discuss the epistemological assumptions that are foundational to life history as we know it. For example, there has been a lot of talk lately about the fluid nature of knowing (Clifford, 1997; Hwu, 1998; Kaplan, 1996; Pinar, 1998; Serres, 1993; Serres with Latour, 1995). Hwu (1998) describes the knowing subject and identity formation as ongoing, emergent, re-created and reconstituted in relationship with others. How does this relate to life history as a research method? From my own experiences with life history method and the recent literature, it is clear that this methodology requires an investigation of the underlying epistemological assumptions. Blurring the boundaries between narrative and life history, Hatch and Wisniewski (1995) present the results of a survey of researchers that emphasized the importance of self-reflective subjectivity, contextualization and life history as a more ethical representation responding to the crisis of representation (Marcus and Fischer, 1986). However, they moved on to highlight the importance of rethinking 'self' through a poststructural analysis that suggests a nonlinear, noncoherent self. This turn requires an epistemological re-positioning in mainstream life history research:

> Individual constructions of 'self' or of 'a life' were seen as complex, situational, fragmented, nonunitary, nonlinear, noncoherent, and constantly in flux. Since individuals' expressions of self and their stories of their lives are the data of narrative and life history inquiries, the poststructual critique must be reconciled by scholars doing this kind of research in the postmodern moment (Hatch and Wisniewski, 1995, p. 122).

This anti-essentialist approach to life history does not go far enough, however. For even as the authors call for an increased awareness of a postmodern identity in flux and a focus on ethics, they fail to problematize the desire for totality that continues to frame life history research. They do provide a useful list of terms that have been used interchangeably in this type of research, such as: life story, storied narrative and oral narrative. Ultimately, however, they continue to utilize a progressivist notion of time:

> Let me say a word on the idea of progress. We conceive of time as an irreversible line, whether interrupted or continuous, of acquisitions and inventions. We go from generalizations to discoveries, leaving behind us a trail of errors finally corrected—like a cloud of ink from a squid. "Whew! We've finally arrived at the truth." It can never be demonstrated whether this idea of time is true or false (Serres with Latour, 1995, p. 48).

Progressivist notions of time deny a multifaceted nature of knowing. Serres with Latour (1995) go on to highlight the fluid nature of time, space and self as relational. For life history as a method to move beyond the myth of totality, it requires researcher recognition of the confluence of fluxes that create it:

> What I seek to form, to compose, to promote—I can't quite find the right word—is a *syrrhèse*, a confluence not a system, a mobile confluence of fluxes. Turbulences, overlapping cyclones and anticyclones, like on the weather map. Wisps of hay tied in knots. An assembly of relations. Clouds of angels passing. Once again, the flames' dance. The living body dances like that, and all life. Weakness and fragility mark the spot of their most precious secret. I seek to assist the birth of an infant (Serres with Latour, 1995, p. 122).

Life history projects often reflect a sense of victory or triumph (as presented later in Irene's story). Research has often focused on non-contradictory truth that is beneficial to society (Serres with Latour, 1995). The search for 'truth' in life history research continues to frame the method as a realist tale.

> Once upon a time men were mobile, errant adventurers, heroes, half-gods or born of men; and in those days they traveled through dangerous lands and rivers, through meadows of asphodel and the fire of God. By strength or ingenuity they would overcome a thousand obstacles, or span in an instant the distances between Earth and heaven. In any event, they were required either to defy death or to seek salvation by pursuing a life of charity (Serres with Latour, 1995, p. 72).

Rethinking life history from a poststructural perspective raised ethical and epistemological issues of representation and highlighted the limits/failures of representation. Lather (1998) talks of the demand in research in curriculum to center such concepts as 'empathy,' 'voice,' and 'authenticity.' "This demand is troubled by critiques of the coherent subject that presuppose the subject who speaks for themselves; the subject capable of knowing others; and the subject in charge of their desires and identifications" (p. 1). It seemed that traditional conceptualizations of life history as discussed above remained mired in realist notions of 'authentic voice' and the fully knowable subject. Therefore, I suggested that studying the authorizing fictions from a poststructuralist perspective could be useful in highlighting obscured discursive power relations through articulating the limits and possibilities of the method.

I attempted to rethink the method as a way of living with ambiguity. The unexpected story, one of four in my master's thesis, forced me to question my authorial/authorizing position and led me to ask—how can I do 'justice' to Irene's story? The remaining life stories were not 'unexpected.' They were expected/anticipated. I was very comfortable with the way the stories provided connections and themes that allowed me to make tentative conclusions. However, these particular stories did not lead me to question the method. "There is a tendency to avoid the difficult story, to want to restore the good name of research with these 'new' and 'better' methods" (Lather, 1998, p. 2–3). For this reason, I focused on the story that made me uncomfortable. I only discuss one story here as I ask—how can I do justice to my participant's voice and life history as she presented it to me, situate it in a sociocultural context and also trouble the contemporaneity of the story as a sociocultural product—all the while as I try to respect her 'voice'? And, what do we do with 'unexpected stories'? Sullivan (1996) discusses the ways in which postcolonial and feminist critiques of ethnography, as a method of representation, have led to the question of ethical rather than epistemological issues. "What gives her the right to speak for another, to tell another's story? If this 'what' is the academy itself, or knowledge itself, or research itself, then isn't the story she tells merely another chapter in the West's master narrative, in its grand story of discovery, appropriation, domestication, assimilation?" (Sullivan, 1996, p. 104). Sullivan highlights an important fact—historicizing life history as a research method and the ways in which the authorizing fictions make possible the re-presentation of participant's stories, one may work to highlight the ways in which foundational assumptions of social scientific research are embedded within a redemptive culture (Popkewitz, 1998c). Thus, when it comes to storysharing (Barone, 1995) or contextualizing life story as called for by Goodson (1995, 1998) the 'voices' of those previously silenced in the research literature (teachers, students, marginalized social groups) are speaking from socially constructed spaces within a redemptive culture.

Therefore, both researcher and researched are authorized, fictionalized *and* normalized thus creating tensions within representation. The next step for life history research is to address the epistemological assumptions and authorizing fictions made possible by the redemptive culture of social and educational research.

> However, for the redemptive culture to function, the teacher and child are naturalized as objects to be rescued. Systemic reform treats different actors as undifferentiated groups or individuals who make their own knowledge and negotiate their own meanings. The knowledge of the teacher, however, is reclassified and turned into the data that the researcher divides and interprets to give voice. The psychologization of the problem-solving individual that is found in the constructivist pedagogies of systemic school reform as well as talk about 'personal knowledge' and 'teacher's wisdom' is the researcher's inscription of the agent. Further, the narratives constructed are neither personal or grounded, but constructed through particular systems of rationalization produced through academic systems of problem solving. This is neither good nor bad, in and of itself. But the 'wisdom of the teacher' assumes a single, universal, and ahistorical field of representation to reality (Popkewitz, 1998c, p. 16).

Therefore, apart from the authorizing fictions of possibilities for the re-presentation of story, the notions of voice and collaboration need to be addressed as fictions also. The naturalizing of teacher voice in the redemptive culture of life history research obscures the effects of power and must be problematized to highlight the way in which it is socially and politically inscribed as technology of power (Popkewitz, 1998c). Life history is always already fiction. Therefore, "from a deconstructionist perspective, the 'double-bind' of identity is always already a struggle within the subject" (Hwu, 1998, p. 23). Below, I re-present a life history that arose from my own research in 1995. As you read through it consider the ways in which the authorizing fictions and normalizing processes of educational research not only make this possible but also limit any attempt to totalize or conclude the story. Situating the method in this way highlights the limits of the research yet moves beyond it to describe the im/possibilities of representation, such as the notions of collaboration and voice. Lather (1998) describes the messy text of *Troubling the Angels* (Lather and Smithies, 1997) as one example of an

The Methodological Journey

uncooperative text that disrupts the authorizing fictions using de-authorizing moves:

> In a book less argued than enacted, Chris and I have written an 'uncooperative text' that refuses mimetic desire and reader entitlement to know. It constructs a distance between reader and subject of the research, producing a kind of gap between text and reader. Refusing the liberal embrace of empathy that reduces otherness to sameness within a personalized culture, declining the too easy to possess knowledge and casting doubt on our capacity to know, it refuses the mutuality and dialogue that typify an empathetic approach to understanding (Lather, 1998, p. 4–5).

A Selection of Life History Data and Analysis.

> *Irene: In a nutshell I was a very messed up person. Probably until 17 years ago and even longer. I never talked to anyone about it, because I just believed it was my fault (Irene, pseudonym).*

At the time of this study Irene was a 39 years old, studying full-time while supporting a husband and four children. She was completing an undergraduate degree in social studies teacher education. I was 'investigating' the ways in which the social studies perspectives of preservice teachers were reflected in their life histories. Irene's story was totally unexpected. Irene stated that it was time to tell her story—too many similar stories were never heard. Her agenda was to break her own silence as a survivor of childhood sexual abuse and substance addiction. What was my agenda? I was doing my master's research and had not fully considered the possibilities of uncovering stories of abuse and resistance through life history interviews. The questions in the structured interviews led to a discussion of the life history of the participants including biographical questions, schooling experiences, formative incidents, belief systems, and social studies perspectives. But instead of the stories that I 'expected,' or hoped to hear, Irene began immediately to disrupt my preconceived notions of life history.

> *Irene: As long as I can remember I began overdosing on drugs and things in school and yet even though I missed a lot of school, my marks were good.... Teachers did not seem to focus on students when their grades were so good. I couldn't trust anyone except my father. I really believed that I wouldn't be happy until my mother was dead.*

Irene's Story is multiply layered: daughter, victim, student, drug addict, wife, missionary, mother, teacher and research participant. From a position of power as research participant, Irene was articulate in her desire to tell her story of resistance and she used this opportunity to present a story of becoming. Maxine Greene (1995) highlights life stories as incessantly perspectival:

> Neither my self nor my narrative can have, therefore, a single strand. I stand at the crossing point of too many social and cultural forces; and in any case, I am forever on my way. My identity has to be perceived as multiple, even as I strive towards some coherent notion of what is humane and decent and just. At the same time, amidst this multiplicity, my life project has been to achieve an understanding of teaching, learning, and the many models of education; I have been creating and continue to create a self by means of that project, that model of gearing into the world (p. 1).

My surprise at this remarkable story and victory narrative of overcoming incredible odds to live a 'normal' life, turned into confusion and concern as the story progressed. What was my responsibility as researcher considering the vulnerability of the participant and the story of sexual and substance abuse revealed/constructed through the interview? Luke (1996) states that positionality is most important to highlight, as "in feminisms generally and in feminist pedagogy specifically, the importance of 'positionality' of voice and experience is paramount" (p. 290). My position as researcher and Irene's as 'researched' were not clearly defined. The resulting story highlighted the messiness of methodology. It also highlights the ways in which Irene resisted my own project by telling the story she thought others should hear. She disrupted the myth of neutrality in life history research. Irene's story challenges preconceived notions of teacher and woman, and her story stayed with me and challenged me to journey further as researcher. Greene (1994) says that "there must be spaces for life stories to be articulated and listened to, whether or not those stories live up to the narrative standards prized in the West" (p. 448). Feminist theory may have provided such spaces for dialogue however, the cultural construction of identities as evinced by these voices are not to be taken as representative or universal—that is, all women, all people of color, all gays and lesbians—for it is the individual voice, as multiply situated, that is discussed in this paper. Luke (1996) troubles the trend toward generalizing statements in feminist research by stating:

The Methodological Journey

> Women's complex and multiple identities experienced *in* and *through* the discourses that define feminine gender identity, sexuality, ethnicity, class, or culture suggest that an understanding of women and the concept of femininity cannot be articulated in universal principles, but must come from women's individual voices articulated from specific social and cultural locations (p. 290).

Luke's (1996) statement may be used not only to frame the discussion of Irene's story but also to frame the method of life history and the limits of representation in such narrative research. Life history as discourse provides a specific cultural and social location in a useful way of framing the resultant stories and the interpretation of such stories. I think this informed discussion of researcher *and* participant standpoints and positionality helps to avoid the 'realist tale' (Van Maanen, 1988).

> Irene: I dropped social studies because I hated it in high school. (Laugh). But I did pick it up in Grade 12 but all I remember of social studies in high school was walking into the room and having the board all written up with notes. The class just copied them. We didn't do group work, we didn't do anything like that. I can't even remember who taught social studies. It was not a highlight. The Principal never came to classes, he taught us Algebra through the intercom.

Here we see Irene's negative schooling experiences framing her desire to do something differently as a future Social Studies teacher. Her standpoint at this stage in her story is as a victim of the system as she unfolds her childhood of sexual abuse and negative schooling experiences. She blames the system and has actively used this occasion to present her story of suffering turned triumph as a 'victory narrative':

> Irene: I never really analyzed or thought about what I really wanted to teach before. I knew I wanted to help kids. I wanted to target the kids that get lost in the system....I think that for me the biggest thing I've learned is that I want them to see that they don't have to be constrained by their situation. They don't have to stay, they can get out of it.

Irene's story was disturbing yet hopeful as she described her experiences as a victim of sexual abuse, her fight to overcome substance addictions and her ultimate triumph through working as a missionary in Central America. In her telling of the story she used the margin as a space for resistance. During one member check, she explicitly requested that I present her Story as it was told (an im/possibility?), for she had been silenced too long. As a wife and mother she felt it was time to heal herself and thus provide a story of hope for other victims of abuse and discrimination. hooks (1996) addresses this issue when she discusses marginality as a vital location for counterhegemonic discourse (stories that challenge the male-dominated culture), constructed through words, habits of being, and way of life:

> As such, I was not speaking of a marginality one wishes to lose—to give up or surrender as part of moving into the center—but rather of a site one stays in, clings to even, because it nourishes one's capacity to resist. It offers to one the possibility of radical perspective from which to see and create, to imagine alternatives, new worlds (hooks, 1996, p. 52)

At the time I had grave concerns about presenting Irene's Story as a private discourse made public yet Irene stated that it was her underlying reason for 'telling' the Story. I was concerned with what I saw as the powerlessness and vulnerability of Irene. Yet she perceived it as a place of resistance and counterhegemonic power. "We also have ample evidence that individuals do not passively accept the cultural categories that are presented to them" (Eisenhart, 1995, p 4). Eisenhart (1995) is interested in how the individual situates him/herelf within an institutional context:

> how the individual positions herself or himself in the situation (e.g., as victim or as in charge), how she or he feels about what is happening, and how past experiences are connected to possible selves within an institutional context. In expressing their interpretations, individuals contribute to the material conditions of their ongoing participation and to the cultural models available (Eisenhart, 1995, p. 21).

From this perspective, the subject Self is neither singular nor fixed and power relations that shape the construction of life histories are seen as fluid, unstable, dispersed and mobile (Foucault, 1980). Therefore, considering the localized construction of Self as the effect of power is useful in highlighting the fluid and plural nature of becoming:

> That this subjectivity is so multiply determined explains how we can be constrained and oppressed given social structures and internalized psychological constraints yet can bypass them by self-conscious self-reconstitutive processes. Such a view of the human subject as an embodied conscious process with multiple aspects and contextualized identities

implies that identity politics based on an essentialist singling out of just one of those aspects to reconstitute will not successfully empower individuals (Ferguson, 1996, pp. 122–123).

As Irene concluded:

> We don't go around reflecting on everything and maybe we should do more reflection. So, I think I've learned a little bit about where I stand. I guess the biggest thing I've learned is that what I believe is OK. And there's nothing wrong with it and I don't have to apologize for my strong beliefs on some areas. I think it intensifies your purpose [and] legitimizes your purposes. So in that respect you can more effectively perhaps diagnose what the problem is instead of just knowing something's wrong. I discovered that I did believe something. Sometimes you really don't know what you believe so its good to clarify it....You can do better than you ever imagined. You don't have to become an abuser, you don't have to stay in that situation. So its seeing the potential and defying the odds.

Thus, Irene finishes her story and outlines her perspectives of Social Studies as liberatory in focus (redemptive, possibly). She clearly highlights her motivation for involvement in this study by concluding with her 'message' to students as "seeing the potential and defying the odds." The development of life history research must include an aspect of the mediated, fluid, multiaspected Self. It is then that we may begin to understand how "individuals organize culture is through the 'stories of self' that they express or enact in joining new social settings" (Eisenhart, 1995, p. 5–6). Ultimately, it has been the 'telling' of Irene's Story that taught me most about myself as researcher, the authorizing fictions that en/dis/able life history as a method or 'representation' and the myths that shape this method within a redemptive culture in social science research.

And so, as I was concluding my writing on this particular life history project (Cary, 1999a), I was also working through my doctoral program. It was really no surprise that I found limitations and the need to redefine another methodology in that project.

Extending Ethnography

So the dissertation story goes.... originally I had planned to conduct a postmodern ethnography of a cohort of the social studies education Professional Development School network (PDS). I was interested in the ways in which power circulated and the culture of the PDS was legitimated and the usefulness of Popkewitz's (1998) conceptualization of the culture of redemption as a framework for understanding (Popkewitz, 1998c, p. 2). However, I was shocked when my attempts to gain entry (seemingly unproblematic in initial discussions with the University Professor in 'charge' of the Social Studies PDS) encountered insurmountable problems. On mentioning my desire to conduct a Foucauldian analysis of the way culture traveled in the PDS using the work of Thomas Popkewitz, I was confronted by icy stare and defensive posture. I was asked to elucidate 'clearly and simply' the theoretical underpinnings of my work and why I was interested in using the work of theorists that ultimately suggested that education 'failed' in its goals. This experience of oppositionality raised questions about possibilities of doing critical and deconstructivist research in the field of education and highlighted the control of research by the gatekeepers. Who gets researched? Who has the power and cultural capital to control or hinder critical research efforts? As a result, I learned a valuable lesson. At that time, when asked about 'improving' teacher education or professional development through research I started to worry about successor regimes and radical oppositionality. I saw my work at that time as aimed at 'improving' (or contextualizing) teacher education through a different lens. In this particular instance it was an attempt to historicize the PDS model as a traveling culture using a critical discourse analysis (Fairclough, 1995) of the PDS texts and discussions with individuals involved in the multiple manifestations of the model in the College of Education (at Mid-West State University) in order to highlight their ways of being and experiences with/in the model.

So, I began to develop a theoretical framework that included a poststructuralist/psychoanalytic analysis of the PDS to suggest ways/spaces/places from which to work within and against the normalizing tendencies of any attempt at teacher education. I started investigating particular manifestations of PDS as educational reform in terms of legitimate knowledge and the travels of PDS culture. This study is discussed in detail in chapter three. The focus for this chapter is to highlight the way I began to negotiate methodology. The PDS research enabled me to study the limits of ethnography and writing about the 'new' postmodern ethnography created spaces for interruption and extension.

'New' Postmodern Ethnography. The totalizing assumptions that shaped ethnography as constructing impartial, objective accounts of static cultures and fascinating Others has been under assault for some time. Critiques of traditional ethnographic practices have highlighted the limits of representation and the historical implications for its role in colonial oppression (Visweswaran, 1994; Marcus and Fischer, 1986). Issues of subjectivity, gendered silences and partiality, implications of the colonizing mentality, to name a few, have been highlighted by a number of authors, according to Van Maanen (1995). "Just what is required of ethnography today is by no means clear, and among its producers and consumers alike, restlessness is the norm" (Van Maanen, 1995, p. 2). Therefore, this project highlighted some of these issues and entertained new ways of 'thinking about' ethnography. My dissertation aimed to exist with/in the tensions that are revealed as characteristic of ethnography as a methodological practice (Van Maanen, 1995; Marcus and Fischer, 1986; Geertz, 1983; Behar, 1995). Ethnographic traditions have entrenched the techniques and results of ethnography and although the 'field' is stretching to embrace novel and alternative procedures, there is a real danger of it remaining intact and unchallenged paradigmatically (Van Maanen, 1995). However, the call for new ways of thinking and of doing ethnography reflected a crumbling ideology, opened the field to the exciting possibilities of existing within the tensions of cultural representation (Clifford and Marcus, 1986).

By creating spaces that trouble declarative or official historiographies I hoped to address discursive power relations in the field that influence/shape the culture of PDS as it traveled across schools and universities (Visweswaran, 1994). Throughout, the focus was on the epistemological assumptions of knowing in a state-of-flux to move away from the more static cultural representations in the traditional historical 'official' accounts described by Visweswaran (1994). Therefore, I utilized literature surrounding current methodological debates surrounding ethnography as a method of cultural representation and troubled the foundational realist assumptions of the method by highlighting the tensions that exist within. Central to this discussion was the realization that ethnography is a social practice, a gathering of rhetorical truths shaped by many subjectivities (Van Maanen, 1995). In this light cultures are no longer seen as holistic, static, 'knowable' objects and the dichotomy of object/subject is blurred.

There are many characteristics of this methodology to address: research on how culture travels; the blurring of validity and ethics in 'good' research; and the epistemological assumptions of 'knowing in a state-of-flux.' Highlighting these characteristics was a strategic move. It made it possible to trouble the tendency towards a static, geographically bound culture inscribed in traditional ethnography (Visweswaran, 1994). The tensions of the economies of truth and the production of knowledge within a redemptive culture provided space from which to address the relatively obscured power relations that circulate in the model of teacher education studied—the Professional Development School.

I attempted to trouble the realist assumptions that continue to permeate methodological discussions in the field. Such discussions reveal the scientistic definitions of validity and design and the way they reflect a desire for authentic cultural descriptions and voices from the field. As Lather (1998) states, "[the] argument is that the research of most use is that which addresses how knowledge remains possible given the end of the value free notion of science and the resultant troubling of confidence in the scientific project, a science 'after truth'" (p. 3). So, by developing a hybrid methodology or bricolage (Denzin, 1994) approach in the research design for this project, I aimed to disrupt the notions of neutrality that prescribe the 'truth' and validity of research. The hybrid included the data collection methodology of the 'new' postmodern ethnography and the data analysis methodology of critical discourse analysis. In this way the overarching methodological frame reflected the tensions of the 'new' postmodern ethnography (Van Maanen, 1995; Marcus and Fischer, 1986; Geertz, 1983; Behar, 1995) as a way of troubling definitive, static descriptions of culture and utilized critical discourse analysis of individual interviews and public policy/archival documents to frame both data collection and data analysis in this study within and against the discursive nature of the PDS model.

Why? Because a crisis in ethnography occurred, as discussed earlier. In terms of ethnography as a method, the totalizing assumptions that shaped this practice as constructing impartial, objective accounts of static cultures and fascinating Others was assaulted. Subjectivity, gendered silences, partiality, and the implications of the colonizing mentality, to name a few, have been highlighted by a number of authors, according to Van Maanen (1995). This 'crisis' (which is more of a final realization of the limits of this

The Methodological Journey

methodological practice) led a number of theorists to attempt to reclaim the 'field.' Clifford (1997, 1986), Marcus and Fischer (1986) and Kaplan (1996), among others, tried to redeem the discipline, for ethnography *is* the defining practice of anthropology. They sought redemption not only of the practice, but of the discipline. It is interesting to note the realist assumptions framed as desire for authenticity and accuracy embedded within the following call for different paradigms in ethnography:

> The only way to an accurate view and confident knowledge of the world is through a sophisticated epistemology that takes full account of intractable contradiction, paradox, irony, and uncertainty in the explanation of human activities. This seems to be the spirit of the developing responses across disciplines to what we described as a contemporary crisis of representation (Marcus and Fischer, 1986, p. 15).

So, even as the field began to wonder about new ways of doing ethnography, entrenched traditions continued to haunt the field. At the same time the 'field' was stretching to embrace novel and alternative procedures, there was a real danger of it remaining intact and unchallenged paradigmatically (Van Maanen, 1995). However, the calls for new ways of thinking and of doing ethnography did open the field to the exciting possibilities of existing within the tensions of cultural representation. "My objective is to move away from a declarative or official historiography founded on transparent 'realist' narrative" (Visweswaran, 1994, p. 61).

Ethnography is both a method and a product (Van Maanen, 1995). It has been utilized as a validating technique for ethnographic authority and cultural representation however, recent moves have problematized the taken-for-granted objectivities of this method (Marcus and Fischer, 1986). New questions are now being asked of ethnography. Experimental works are being composed. Many, if not most, of the representational techniques of realist (alternatively, classical) ethnography are now seen by many as dated, naive and, in a certain light, both professionally and socially indefensible (Van Maanen, 1995, p. 12). The realization that ethnography is a social practice (a gathering of rhetorical truths shaped by many subjectivities) framed the dissertation research. In this light, cultures were not seen as holistic, static 'knowable' objects and the dichotomy of object/subject was blurred. In this project, the discourses framing the PDS model at Midwest State University called for a 'new' way of looking at cultural description and a more complex understanding of the location of that description.

Questioning the ethnographic canonical assumptions of 'truth' and 'reality,' traditional practices enabled a 'new' ethnography (postmodern ethnography) to arise. However, just what was this 'new' postmodern ethnography? According to Van Maanen (1995):

> the point driven home in these re-presentations is that the group portrayed is anything but isolated, timeless, or beyond the reach of contemporary society. The wistful assumption of 'one place, one people, one culture' no longer holds the ethnographic imagination in check. This is made quite clear in what Marcus (1994) calls the 'messy texts' of a deterritorialized, open-ended, and 'new' ethnography that attempts to foster an idea of how lives around the globe may be contrasted yet still interconnected. Important messy texts do not lament the loss of the anthropological object but, in fact, invent a more complex object whose study can be as revelatory and as realistic as the old (Van Maanen, 1995, p. 19).

Van Maanen's arguments, however, were in danger of reinscribing the status quo in ethnography as what he "continue[d] to look for is the close study of culture as lived by particular people, in particular places, doing particular things at particular times" (Van Maanen, 1995, p. 23). This was not blurring the realist ontological boundaries enough and contained little awareness of the partial and traveling nature of culture. Marcus (1994), whom Van Maanen credits with the concept of the 'new' ethnography, goes one step further and describes 'messy' texts as the postmodern representation of ethnography. The crisis of representation and incredulity toward metanarratives, according to Marcus, has highlighted new ways of 'doing' ethnography from legitimating "new objects, new styles of research and writing, and a shift in the historic purpose of anthropological research toward its long-standing, but underdeveloped, project of cultural critique" (Marcus, 1994, p. 564). In terms of who coined 'new' ethnography, while Van Maanen (1995) attributed the term to Marcus (1994), Behar (1995) introduced *Women Writing Culture* by crediting Clifford (1986) with the idea. This is complicated further by Clifford's use of the term to refer to the 'new' ethnography of the 1920's in *The Predicament of Culture* in 1988. However, the concept has become representative of the multiple issues arising from the crisis in the practice of ethnography.

So, postmodern ethnography is about living within the tensions of the 'messiness' of the social text. Ethnography in this light can be seen as cultural translation and it is not possible to ever fully assimilate difference. This enables the researcher to address a number of issues, including: what is 'good' ethnographic research; and what are the im/possibilities of fully 'knowing/knowable' a subject?

> The postmodern idea of radical or surplus difference counters the liberal concept with the idea that difference can never be fully consumed, conquered, or experienced, and thus any interpretive framework must remain partly unresolved in a more serious sense than is usually stipulated as 'good manners' in doing interpretive work (Marcus, 1994, p. 566).

Visweswaran (1994) talked of Clifford's work in highlighting the danger of putting all the epistemic weight on fieldwork in ethnography. She then discussed the ruptured understandings evident in feminist ethnography as representative of the disjunctions and gendered misunderstandings of experimental or 'new' ethnography long before the current crisis in ethnography (Visweswaran, 1994, p 29–30). This notion of failure is most important in the new postmodern ethnography and Visweswaran presents the failure of feminist ethnography as central when one considers the fluid and partial nature of knowing the subject/other that may trouble totalizing cultural accounts:

> In this reconstituted feminist project, the practice of failure is pivotal [and] not surprisingly, this historical moment is also marked by the failure of an entire genre of description: ethnography....This notion of ethnographic and epistemic failure influences the practice of feminist fieldwork. For our failures are as much a part of the process of knowledge construction as are our oft-heralded 'successes.' Failure is not just a sign of epistemological crisis (for it is indeed also that), but also, I would argue, an epistemological construct. Failure signals a project that may no longer be attempted, or at least not on the same terms (Visweswaran, 1994, p. 100).

This was most useful because it made it possible for me to reflect on the dangers and difficulties of the critical realist assumptions that framed ethnography so I could revisit the notion of epistemological understanding and highlight the fluidity of knowing of the 'new' postmodern ethnography. As a result, I found the discourses surrounding the PDS model to be fluid and traveling epistemological constructions (as you will see in chapter three).

Epistemology and Location. It's all about epistemology. A constant theme in the literature surrounding the 'new' postmodern ethnography, I discovered, was the partiality of knowing and the challenge to the totalizing tendencies of traditional ethnography as presenting a 'fully knowable' subject. Marcus and Fischer (1986) called for more sophisticated epistemologies and Geertz (1983) talked of the changing culture of thought. This raised conceptual questions about the construction of craft procedures such as ethnography and it opens a world of multiple epistemologies. "The refiguration of social theory represents, or will if it continues, a sea change in our notion not so much of what knowledge is but of what it is we want to know" (Geertz, 1983, p. 34). As a result, there was a general call for epistemological debates within the practice of ethnography. "The development of ethnographic science cannot ultimately be understood in isolation from more general political-epistemological debates about writing and the representation of otherness" (Clifford, 1988, p. 24). Writing, translation, multiple subjectivities and political constraints have given ethnographic authority to the writer and has resulted in the ethnographer as the being classically presented as the "purveyor of truth in the text" (Clifford, 1988, p. 25). Classically, ethnography involved a search for origins and the innovations of the 1920's validated an efficient ethnography that was based on scientific participant observation and employed a special relationship with the 'subject' as an absolute while transforming cultural ambiguities and diversities into an integrated portrait (Clifford, 1988, pp. 32–40). However, Clifford called for a new way of reading and writing ethnography against the grain that "is not yet authoritative in those specific ways that are now politically and epistemologically under question" (Clifford, 1988, pp. 45, 53). His elucidation of the ethnography of the 1920's (the classical ethnography of Malinowski and Mead) included the privileging of fieldwork. Fieldwork was seen as the distinguishing feature of anthropological ethnography and stays of at least one year were typical. Thus dwelling became privileged over travel through the emphasis on the site or location and not on the movement to or from the sites studied. The transport of the ethnographer and the cultural representation were erased as the main focus was on participant observation that enables the holistic experience of all the seasons and festivities of the annual cycle within a contained geographic area (Clifford, 1988). "It is now widely understood that the old localizing strategies—by bounded *community*, by organic *culture*, by *region*, by *center and periphery*—may obscure as much as they reveal" (Clifford, 1997, p. 245).

The Methodological Journey 43

This epistemological turn also blurred the issues of location and site in ethnographic representation. Clifford (1997) developed this idea in his work on dwelling as opposed to travel in ethnography. "Fieldwork has always been a mix of institutionalized practices of dwelling and traveling. But in the disciplinary idealization of the 'field,' spatial practices of moving to and from, in and out, passing through, have tended to be subsumed by those of dwelling (rapport, initiation, familiarity)" (Clifford, 1997, p. 67–68). Clifford (1997) moved on to discuss the concept of habitus as arising from feminist research that enabled a move beyond spatial and chronological prescriptions and cautions us to be aware of concretizing travel and habitus embodied cultural experiences as ethnographers continue to search for cultural origins and authentic understanding are extremely important in the 'new' postmodern ethnography. This was important as otherwise exclusivist paradigms would be uninterrupted and the imposition of strict meanings within the search for authenticity would continue.

> The epistemology this implies cannot be reconciled with a notion of cumulative scientific progress, and the partiality at stake is stronger than the normal scientific dictates that we study problems piecemeal, that we must not overgeneralize, that the best picture is built up by an accretion of rigorous evidence. Cultures are not 'scientific' objects (assuming such things exist, even in the natural sciences). Culture, and our views of 'it,' are produced historically, and are actively contested. There is no whole picture that can be 'filled in,' since the perception and filling of a gap lead to the awareness of other gaps (Clifford, 1986, p. 18).

Culture is neither static nor stagnant. The situated, partial and contingent epistemological assumptions that this implies are vital as there is no historical location from which a "full comparative account could be produced" (Clifford, 1997, p. 11). There is no authentic site. Serres with Latour (1995) converse at length about science, culture and time in a state-of-flux that addresses the partial knowing of the 'new' postmodern ethnography. The traditional totalizing nature of realist epistemologies are highlighted as follows:

> We are accustomed to abstraction via concepts, to concepts from one area organizing the totality of everything. Which explains the smugness surrounding those who continually repeat 'the ontology of Being,' 'Ideas,' or 'categories,' with references to the 'knowing subject,' 'the analysis of language,' and so on—as though it were always a matter of constructing (or

tearing down) a very solid edifice, whose peak or foundation would organize all stability (Serres with Latour, 1995, p. 112).

Time and geographic locale as valorized in the ethnography of the 1920's inscribed a realist, static and linear epistemological conceptualization. By conceiving of time and space as fluid, with fluctuating boundaries and edges, the 'new' postmodern ethnography made it possible to move beyond simplistic representations and respond to the ethnographic crisis. This epistemological transformation required a 'state-of-flux' philosophy, such as described in the work of Michel Serres (1993). Destabilizing and disrupting essentialist assumptions provides possibilities for other ways of knowing. Bringing together time and 'networks of knowing' challenged ethnographers to an increased awareness of the fluctuation and bifurcation of cultural understanding. In this way progressivist notions of culture that have been immersed within linear time analyses are deconstructed and the search for an authentic 'truth' is interrupted. Once it has been accepted that cultures are not static but fluid and the im/possibilities of fully knowing the subject are highlighted, cultural representation becomes more complicated.

Traveling Culture and Home. Throughout my life and in my research, issues of travel and home have always been central. Colonialization through historic misuses of research and progress are also major issues in any contemporary approach to research. Moving our focus from the field to home, or from static representations to traveling discourses and cultures is an important move here.

A variety of concepts are presented in this section as theorists grapple with the notion of motion-filled cultures. From Clifford's (1992, 1997) traveling culture to Pratt's (1992) contact zones, the field is struggling to move beyond totalizing static notions of culture. For example, Clifford (1988, 1992, 1997) valorizes travel as the 'missing link ' of ethnographic practice, whereas Gilroy (1993) utilizes the diasporic nature of the black Atlantic to disrupt the modernist notions of absolute and static cultures. Bhabha (1994) launches into a highly theoretical discussion of the location of culture also with reference to diasporic notions of culture and emphasizes cultural difference—not cultural diversity. Pratt (1992) (the only woman in *Writing Culture*) employs historical texts which have been marginalized as 'travel writing' and describes the concept of 'contact zones' as a space/place of cultural hybridity. Kaplan (1996) and Dubois (1995) take a more

The Methodological Journey

critical stance in the travel debate wheras Pratt (1992) talks of the colonial expansionism described and reinscribed through travel writing. She discusses how travel writing and the Enlightenment natural history project produced the 'planetary' consciousness or Eurocentric global awareness. The imperialist foundations of the authority of travel writers is conceptualized as the 'monarch-of-all-I-survey' (Pratt, 1992, p. 201). This masculinist authority continued to develop, as discovery and expansionism went hand in hand. A major contribution to the understanding of the interactive and heterogeneous nature of culture is presented in Pratt's concept of the 'contact zone.' This refers to the "space of colonial encounters, the space in which peoples geographically and historically separated come into contact with each other and establish ongoing relations, usually involving conditions of coercion, radical inequality, and intractable conflict" (Pratt, 1992, p. 6). Pratt (1992) highlights the celebratory absolutist project of the colonial expansion as indicative of the Othering that has become traditional in ethnographic representations. Classic tropes of Utopia and Dystopia are revealed in the historical texts of travel writers. Pratt's study of travel writing adds to the understanding that cultures are interactively form/ed/ing and suggests an interrogation of the authorial stance may challenge the imperialist nature of ethnographic writing.

Bhabha (1994) and Gilroy (1993) use the postmodern moment to disrupt absolutist notions of cultural location. Using concepts of 'beyond' and 'in-between,' Bhabha identifies a theoretically innovative move to focus on moments and processes as cultural constructions: "These 'in-between' spaces provide the terrain for elaborating strategies of selfhood—singular or communal—that initiate new signs of identity, and innovative sites of collaboration, and contestation, in the act of defining the idea of society itself" (Bhabha, 1994, p. 2). Bhabha (1994) moves beyond simplistic discussions of travel and engages the reader in the metaphorical nature of travel and location:

> If, in our traveling theory, we are alive to the *metaphoricity* of the peoples of imagined communities—migrant or metropolitan—then we shall find the space of the modern nation-people is never simply horizontal. Their metaphoric movement requires a kind of 'doubleness' in writing: a temporality of representation that moves between cultural formations and social processes without a centered causal logic. And such cultural movements disperse the homogenous, visual time of the horizontal society. The secular language of interpretation needs to go beyond the horizontal

critical gaze if we are to give 'the nonsequential energy of lived historical memory and subjectivity' its appropriate narrative authority. We need another time of *writing* that will be able to describe the ambivalent and chiasmatic intersections of time and place that constitute the problematic 'modern' experience of the Western nation (Bhabha, 1994, p. 141).

The diasporic nature of culture is an important move beyond the essentialist tendencies of traditional ethnography. However, the many-sitedness of diasporic cultures, such as the black Atlantic described in Gilroy's (1993) work, also challenges the color-blind nature of discussions of traveling cultures. He attempts to provide an open-ended discussion on particular aspects, yet he has also been criticized for the privileging of African-origins in his work (Kaplan, 1996) and for the masculinist tendencies of his work by Clifford (1997). It is vitally important, however, to include his work in any discussion of the postmodern turn toward cultural 'motion-ness'. Gilroy (1993) presents specific historical events as evidence of the literal movement of the black culture in diaspora, but he does tend to essentializing black culture and is in danger of totalizing the diaspora itself:

> The specificity of the modern political and cultural formation I want to call the black Atlantic can be defined, on one level, through this desire to transcend both the structures of the nation state and the constraints of ethnicity and national particularity. These desires are relevant to understanding political organising and cultural criticism. They have always sat uneasily alongside the strategic choices forced on black movements and individuals embedded in national political cultures and nation states in America, the Caribbean, and Europe (Gilroy, 1993, p. 19).

The danger of romanticizing the diaspora moves the discussion away from possible cultural understanding to the critical stance of political struggle. This tendency adds to the danger of reinscribing the realist ontological assumptions that culture is in fact static but was 'forced' to move diasporically (i.e., involuntary immigration versus voluntary immigration). However, Gilroy manages to move beyond this to emphasize the hybridity of culture through his mapping of the transnational and transethnic domain (Kaplan, 1996, p. 134). Bhabha (1994), like Gilroy (1993), refers to the diaspora yet he takes us a step further in his analysis of the political and historical, although it seems as if race has been downplayed in this discussion. Diaspora is seen here as social construction and cultural production that highlights the ethnocentricity of the 'knowable' subject:

The Methodological Journey

> The wider significance of the postmodern condition lies in the awareness that the epistemological 'limits' of those ethnocentric ideas are also the enunciative boundaries of a range of other dissonant even dissident histories and voices—women, the colonized, minority groups, the bearers of policed sexualities. For the demography of the new internationalism is the history of the diaspora, the major social displacements of peasant and aboriginal communities, the poetics of exile, the grim pose of political and economic refugees (Bhabha, 1994, pp. 4–5).

Clifford (1997) describes in detail how the diasporic discourses are counterhegemonic and they fail to claim purity or authenticity, but rather highlight the complicity of the utopia and dystopia binary of cultural development and representation (p. 265). In any case, Bhabha's powerful concept of cultural hybridity and Gilroy's diasporic interpretations of culture disrupt previous attempts to contain and describe cultures as static, unified and authentic. Therefore, we can move on to consider Kaplan's (1996) critical interpretation of traveling theories from a feminist perspective. As a student of Clifford's, she is immersed within the idea of travel yet attempts to use academic distance to critique the work in this area. She asks many important questions and highlights the privileged nature of travel theorizing and the use of metaphors and symbols to present such cultural displacement as individualized and elitist (Kaplan, 1996, p. 4). As a synthesis of work in this area her text is very useful. The concepts of exile and tourist are investigated as romanticized Western notions of travel that have constructed the Other through the legitimization of social reality in such binaries as:

- First/Third worlds
- metropolitan/rural, and
- development/underdevelopment (Kaplan, 1996).

The desire for authenticity is highlighted as central to the modernist project: "Articulated as a binary between pure travel and tourism, such modernisms reproduce metaphors of space and place that signal the vibrant hold of Eurocentric conceptions of national, cultural, and racial differences on supposedly progressive theories of culture and politics" (Kaplan, 1996, p. 85). She also discusses the origin of the term 'politics of location' as a North American feminist articulation of difference that emphasizes, interrogates and deconstructs the position, identity and privilege of whiteness (Kaplan, 1996, p. 163).

Kaplan (1996) states, "The crucial questions remain: Who writes of difference, location, and travel? And who gains?" (p. 169). This move makes it possible to raise the question of privilege and position in the authorizing practices of traditional ethnography and highlights the danger of ignoring the same tensions within postmodern ethnography. She goes on to criticize Clifford's (1992, 1997) work as seeking greater ethnographic authority through a 'play' on language however, she supports his challenge to the universalist assumptions of travel when he juxtaposes 'dwelling' with the more Eurocentric concept of 'nomad' to create a site of resistance to the imperialist gaze (Kaplan, 1996). Ultimately, Kaplan (1996) highlights the tensions and the unresolved nature of cultural hybridity, fluidity and the politics of location and her work brings a lot of the contemporary literature in this area and the open-endedness of her critique is aimed to stimulate possibilities for a move beyond the confines of the modernist foundations of travel theorizing:

> This form of critical practice identifies the grounds for historically specific differences and similarities among women in diverse and asymmetrical relations, creating alternative histories, identities, and possibilities for alliances. Such a politics of location undermines any assertion of progressive, singular development and alerts us to the interpellation of the past in the present. A politics of location in this mode critiques the limits of modernity without overvalorizing the possibilities of postmodernity (Kaplan, 1996, p. 187).

Her work is important as an attempt to highlight the lack of consensus in the field that presents possibilities for new ways of writing and reading culture as sociohistorical and political constructs.

Along the same lines Dubois (1995) describes the constructedness of travel as always already inscribed socially, historically and politically. He challenges Clifford's (1992) celebration of travel as central to 'new' ethnography by presenting "the process of travel, sought out as a release from constricting traditions and ways of life—as a release from the prescribed—is inevitably prescribed as well as inscribed in a tradition of travel writing of which anthropology is a part" (Dubois, 1995, p. 307). He also discussed the masculinist assumptions surrounding the subdiscipline of travel in anthropology:

> Through a doubled exploration that moves between theoretical discussions and autobiography, I trace the outlines of a white, male tradition of travel, which, while it has become universalized in much anthropological discourse, actually has a set of very specific characteristics and modes of

transmission. I speak about this tradition as one wrapped up within it, appreciating its possibilities but increasingly wary of naturalizing them as fundamental experiences (Dubois, 1995, p. 309).

James Clifford is often presented as the ultimate 'travel' anthropologist yet his work has been challenged by many of the theorists discussed previously. Clifford (1997) sees the future of the discipline as problematic as he struggles to exist in the 'postmodern.' However, in *Routes: Travel and Translation in the Late Twentieth Century*, Clifford (1997) presents a new genre. The authority of his voice in this 'field' of travel writing is strong and vital—the 'Father' of travel. Yet, whereas Kaplan attempts to deconstruct the metaphors of travel and displacement in postmodern ethnography, Clifford prefers to engage in a narrative approach stemming from his own travels and the representations of culture in museums:

During the course of this work, *travel* emerged as an increasingly complex range of experiences: practices of crossing and interaction that troubled the localism of many common assumptions about culture. In these assumptions authentic social existence is, or should be, centered in circumscribed places—like the gardens where the word 'culture' derived its European meanings. Dwelling was understood to be the local ground of collective life, travel a supplement; roots always precede routes. But what would happen, I began to ask, if travel were untethered, seen as a complex and pervasive spectrum of human experiences. Practices of displacement might emerge as *constitutive* of cultural meanings rather than as their simple transfer or extension (Clifford, 1997, p. 3).

The extent to which it is possible to rethink ethnography as a methodology grounded in realist assumptions of participant observations is the issue here. Clifford admits that the normative power of ethnographic practice remains (Clifford, 1997, p. 72). While there is no doubt that he is contributing to the field, tensions remain that go beyond his eloquent narrative to the practice of ethnographic methodologies and cultural representation (translation/interpretation) in the postmodern. Notions of partiality and ambiguity are indicative of the open-endedness and many-sidedness of the crisis of representation in ethnography yet Clifford (1997) suggests a unidisciplinary approach when he states that: "Travel, redefined and broadened, will remain constitutive of fieldwork, at least in the near term. This will be necessary for institutional and material reasons. Anthropology must preserve not only its disciplinary identity but also its credibility with scientific institutions and funding sources"

(Clifford, 1997, p. 89). I have found his work to be very useful. I discuss his work on travel and 'home' in more detail in chapter five in a postcolonial moment, and I have also utilized this rethinking of 'home' as beyond boundaries and in a state-of-flux in the research on juvie girls I discuss in Chapter four.

Therefore, postmodern ethnography as theorized here, enabled or demanded a move beyond simplistic notions of knowing, culture, travel and home. That is why I found it so useful. This move became embedded in my construction of a research theory. It highlighted that we know what we know is fluid and traveling and it was an especially important addition to the journey of understanding on a number of fronts (e.g., the historic and colonializing dangers of research and the consumption of the other in knowledge projects emerged as central). I have attempted to bring together theories from a number of fields to address the lack of analytical frameworks in educational research and the need for the study of the discursive production of knowing. This is my response to what I perceive to be a real problem in educational research. That is, the need to connect our data analysis with our theoretical frames and the big picture of the field we often relegate to our literature reviews. In the next section, I present a more recent wondering.

Positionality

Recently, another research issue came to my attention. I began to consider that positionality as a methodological strategy was not enough in educational research to reveal and address the oppressive tendencies and privileges inherent within. I felt positionality was in danger of becoming a 'quick and easy' fix to the problem of the responsibility and the inherent problem of the colonizing power of the researcher, as discussed above. In 2002, I began a study of a charter school aimed at 'Push-Out Recovery' in central Texas and I talk about that in detail in chapter four. As I have mentioned, I was expecting stories of exclusion and redemption however, the unexpected stopped me in my tracks—again (Cary, 1999a). It was so much more complicated than that. And positioning my response and my expectations as a privileged, White researcher was not enough to work with. My concern was that my concern with my embedded privilege required more attention than the structuralist tool of positionality provided. I needed to investigate embedded epistemology, such as outlined by St. Pierre (2000). Indeed, Pillow (2000) called for exemplars of postmodern research and I began to see that my project was just that. I had intended a study of subject negotiation and educational discourses and found instead that I had to go far deeper in my analysis than I expected—in order to address the oppressive tendencies of educational research. This section, therefore, suggests that positionality was not enough—to understand the complexities of the research situation and the response it called forth in me. I realized that the most important issues were epistemological—how the students knew the Charter School and how I knew the Charter School. Not meaning-making but knowing. As I have said many times, it is all about how we know what we know.

In recent years there has been a move in critical and postmodern research to address issues of positionality and epistemology in educational research (Roman, 1993; Villenas, 1996; St. Pierre, 2000; Pillow, 2000). It is interesting that these closely related frames or issues are often separated in such discussions. In order to move the field beyond positionality, toward a more complicated understanding of the way epistemology shapes all research (regardless of paradigm), this will highlight the historical moment of positionality as a structuralist tool and more recent moves in the field. The issue is—positionality is not enough, and separate discussions of epistemology are often not connected to the actual work of educational researchers. Epistemological discussions seem to live alone in the rarified atmosphere of foundational or philosophical discussions. To this end, I believe that this book and the Curriculum Spaces Research Theory responds to the call by St. Pierre (2000) to present a number of exemplars of embedded epistemological investigations. Beginning researchers should understand the historical concept of positionality and connected issues, such as; etic/emic perspectives, the colonizing tendencies of research, and the crisis of representation (Roman, 1993; Villenas, 1996; McRobbie, 1991; Clifford, 1986). However, the current historically inscribed moment calls for increased rigor in educational research and I present this avant-garde research theory as one way of complicating the way we know research by responding to Pillow's (2000) call.

The move toward positionality emerged about twenty years ago in structuralist research, specifically, feminist research and then more general critical research (Roman, 1993). What has emerged had often been the discussion of positionality as it occurred in the 'field' and confessional narratives that often erase the participants and the study itself. Actually, positionality as a tool in structuralist research was part of a much larger debate that centered issues of the historical, social and political nature of knowledge and the illustrative function of research (Lather, 1986). In this way, positionality became a vital move in critical educational research that reminded the researcher of their 'power-full' positions in the interpretive and translated nature of qualitative research (Marcus and Fischer, 1986). "To put it briefly, *representations* are *interpretations*. They can never be mirror images.... This is intrinsically neither good nor bad, but it does have consequences that must be recognized" (McRobbie, 1991, p. 69).

As such, it was one of the most important turns in educational research and should remain a central issue in research from the critical (including feminist and critical race research). Roman (1993), referred to this as double exposure:

> Like the visual image to which it refers, the dialectic of double exposure may be used by feminist materialist ethnographers to self-consciously and reflexively expose how their prior beliefs and structural (class, gender, and racial) interests partially constitute the empirical evidence for or against their descriptions and analyses of the research subjects" (Roman, 1993, p. 280–281).

However, this historic structuralist tool has its limits and I suggest here that a postmodern perspective is useful as it offers ways to extend or complicate it further. Thus, we can continue to reveal the dangers of the oppressive tendencies of educational research. Positionality as it stands often remains in the realm of field work:

> The field roles and rhetorical stances that establish the 'going native' and 'being a fly on the wall' approaches to participant-observation vary with the degree to which researchers openly disclose to research subjects their purposes in conducting their studies. Yet with either approach, researchers frequently justify their method as the most unobtrusive and inconspicuous means of eliciting intimate insights and responses from research subjects, enabling the ethnographer to tease out culturally specific yet tacit understandings which otherwise would remain undisclosed" (Roman, 1993, p. 282—283).

We must work to address the contemporary concerns that the failure or limits of positionality emerge in realist, descriptive, confessional and redemptive data narratives (Lather, 1986;

The Methodological Journey

Popkewitz, 1998c). Positionality is paradigm bound and I wonder if something is missing—and thus I call for a move to a place where *all* research takes into account the ways of knowing that shape a project—from nuts to bolts. One way to address this failure is to move the discussion to the complicated understanding of epistemology that includes gendered, raced and sexualized knowing.

> Epistemological choices about who to trust, what to believe, and why something is true are not benign academic issues. Instead, these concerns tap the fundamental question of which versions of truth will prevail and shape thought and action (Collins, 1991, p. 203).

I think it is vital to move the discussion of positionality forward to include epistemological perspectives, not just as a perspective, but as an active part of the research process that shapes everything from the choice of topic, to the questions and, finally, to the conclusions (Pillow, 2000). It is time to move into a more holistic position—and force the issue that epistemological concerns shape every part of the process (a fact understood twenty years ago—but sometimes lost in the positionality fervor that followed. We have been inundated with confessional narratives—most often by White researchers attempting to situate their privileged raced knowing in the research process. But it is not enough. It is also not enough to understand that etic/emic (outsider/insider) positions seem to create hierarchies of knowing that suggest authentic insider knowing is more valid and less suspect. As Villenas (1996) cautions, even the 'native' ethnographer is not innocent: "This 'native' ethnographer is potentially both the colonizer, in her university cloak, and the colonized, as a member of the very community that is made 'other' in her research" (Villenas, 1996, p. 712). She goes on to suggest that all researchers are implicated as colonizers when they claim authenticity of interpretation and the authority of knowing. This highlights the danger in claiming, whether it is a claim of epistemological authenticity or authority as a result of gendered, raced or classed positionalities. We must remind ourselves that we are talking about epistemological connections and considerations—not innocence.

All knowing is suspect, however, not all knowing is equal. This is not a discussion about relativism. We must definitely situate race, gender and other ways of knowing in qualitative research—we just need to do it in a more complicated and sophisticated manner—to avoid the convenient escape from responsibility regarding the embedded nature of privilege and the colonizing oppressive tendencies of research. This is not a call for such research to cease—rather it is a call for a more rigorous stance in critical and post-critical research. Therefore, we need to add to epistemological discussions the element of action and move positionality into the next millennium. Then the doing/knowing/framing/shaping/analyzing/concluding will be all inclusive in this struggle.

As discussed earlier, Pillow (2000) highlights the question that method is not the issue. It is an epistemological issue we should discuss. In response to Constas (1998) she states that this is central in a postmodern perspective: "How can we ignore the epistemological challenges in postmodern theory and still understand postmodern research? We cannot, just as simply one cannot separate the epistemologies of feminist or race theory from their methodological and epistemological practices" (Pillow, 2000, p. 22–23). I resonated with this article as an example of what postmodern educational research might be and how it addressed the lack or failure of positionality across the boundaries of the paradigms (Pillow, 2000). This is about the ethics of research. St. Pierre (2000) reminds us:

> I suggest this ethical approach holds for whatever kind of educational research we undertake, using whatever epistemologies we become attached to—positivism, postmodernism, liberal humanism, queer theories… This kind of inquiry, then, is always already political, ethical, and material since it does not stray far from the lived experiences of those influenced by educational research. To this end, I believe that our responsibility is to keep educational research in play, increasingly unintelligible to itself, in order to produce different knowledge and produce knowledge differently as we work for social justice in the human sciences (St. Pierre, 2000, p. 27).

Final Thoughts

So, I think the next step calls for more than positionality and more than discourse analysis. It is a call to connect theoretical frames and the analysis of discourse. I suggest that we need to look carefully at the desires that inhabit our research and the social and educational discourses that frame our knowing. Educational research is not innocent of epistemic violence. And we need to work more carefully, with greater attention to the ethics of knowing that emerge in the research relationship. I attempted to address these issues in my most

The Methodological Journey

recent research with the Charter School. It helped to solidify the study of individual subject positions, how discourses play out (or travel) in educational institutions, reform movements, and social and educational discourses. It is then possible to create spaces of emancipation and equity by revealing the contingent forms of knowledge and power in which we are all embedded. This has been an attempt to highlight the effects of power in a more complicated way. Every step of the project was framed by my way of knowing the charter school. The students interrupted this. My White researcher privilege demanded more than a positionality discourse. It required an analytical frame that revealed the embedded knowing that framed the project. This knowing was privileged, raced, classed and gendered. The social and educational discourses that shape our knowing as researchers are always already in danger of colonizing and oppressing. Thus, I have journeyed through a number of methodologies over a number of years to develop ways of interrupting, extending and redefining how we 'do' research and how we know ourselves and our participants (such as Irene and the students at the Charter School) in the doing of research. In the next three chapters I present a selection of studies that investigated social and educational discourses on three levels, as suggested by Fairclough (1995). Chapter three looks at the societal level; chapter four presents the institutional stories; and chapter five is a more personal, localized knowing project. As discussed earlier, this in no way suggests these levels of the discursive production of knowing are separate or static. Rather, I found it to be a useful way to highlight the different ways one might use the Curriculum Spaces Research Theory.

3
The Good Teacher:
Charter Schools and Teacher Education

This chapter presents two research projects that investigate the discursive production of the 'good teacher' and the exclusions that emerge within the social and educational discourses of schooling. It is a beginning, a way of taking off point for the explication of Curriculum Spaces Research Theory at the level of the societal framing of knowing. Two studies are presented and teacher education reform and charter schools are discussed. McNeil (2000), Valenzuela (1999) and Popkewitz (1998a) discuss the various ways the discourses of schooling exclude and refuse to educate those 'outside' the mainstream, as a result of cultural, societal and socioeconomic factors. Curriculum Spaces Research Theory is used to reveal how the discursive production of the 'good teacher' in a teacher education reform model and in a charter school setting play out.

It is vital that we begin to understand how our ways of knowing are framed at the societal level. This understanding of the big picture enables us to consider the implicit ways we conform and resist at the level of multiple subjectivities. This chapter presents the findings of a study that investigated the way a particular educational reform movement was framing teacher education at a large midwestern research university. Within the discourses of the reform a number of problematic assumptions about what was good teaching and a desire to professionalize emerged into a rejection of the historically feminized knowing in teaching and a celebration of a masculine scientific model. At the same time, this chapter also presents a brief discussion of the way another reform effort, the Charter School Movement, has framed the way we know education in more recent times. So, the big picture of educational reform in this chapter suggests that in efforts to improve the profession and address equity, we remain embedded within assumptions that normalize teachers and students.

The social and educational discourses that frame the reform movements discussed here, the Professional Development School Model and the Charter School Movement, are neither neutral or natural educational reforms and by drawing upon the Curriculum Spaces Research Theory I was able to reveal the danger of failing to interrogate these normalizing practices and reforms in education. The discourses emerge into and produce reductionist tendencies that govern our mentalities (our ways of being) and this produces exclusivist gendered and raced ways of knowing. These reductions also include legitimized constructions of the various subject positions within the reforms, such as good teacher, good citizen and good student. By highlighting the big picture social and educational discourses, this chapter begins the exemplars of Curriculum Spaces by drawing our attention to the way this plays out at the highest level.

Curriculum Spaces is defined at this level in the broadest sense as I discuss how the spaces in the PDS model of teacher education and the discourses that shape the Charter School Movement illustrate normalizing practices. In this way, they reduce the spaces of being and in effect, maintain dominant constructions that reproduce the status quo despite the best of intentions for 'change' and 'improvement.' It is vital that we study Curriculum Spaces at this level because, if uninterrogated/uninterrupted, such reform efforts will result in reductionist and prescriptive notions of "citizen." This chapter discusses the dangers of assimilationism, the reinscription of whiteness, and the gendered technical rationalist nature of teacher education reform rhetoric. I believe it is time to study the foundational assumptions that frame the way we talk (and act and think) about these areas as a way to highlight and disrupt the dominant knowledge project in social education (Lincoln, 1998). These seemingly disparate reforms intersect at the level of social educational discourses (Popkewitz, 1998a; Fairclough, 1995).

The work of Popkewitz (1998c) has been vital to this project. From my initial concerns with the valorization of the PDS model and the celebration of Charter Schools, I needed a way to step back to see what was at work and how the power regimes played out in these spaces. Drawing upon Popkewitz's (1998c) conception of the redemptive culture of the educational and social sciences as a framework for understanding has provided a provocative positionality for this discussion. Using critical discourse (Fairclough, 1995) and poststructural analyses (Foucault, 1980; Popkewitz, 1998c; Ong, 1999; Britzman, 1998), as outlined in chapter one, I was able to study the multiply-layered discourses in these two seemingly distinct areas and conclude that they are suggestive of a particular conception of citizen and that practices situated as transformational and

The Good Teacher

liberatory are not necessarily so. In conclusion, I was able to immerse myself in the refusals of citizenship as a socially constructed subject position that might limit democratic participation and play out in the way we know/talk/act in social education—the big picture (Cary, 2001).

Although this chapter asks more questions than it answers, it is the beginning of a space for rethinking and questioning unarticulated assumptions about how we come to "know" educational reform at the societal level.

A Postmodern Moment

At the beginning of this discussion it important to frame the Curriculum Space from a theoretical perspective. A number of authors have addressed the discourses that frame the 'social education' space. Stanley (1985, 1992), Lincoln (1998) and Popkewitz (1998a) have discussed ways to rethink social education reform and research in this postmodern moment. They highlight that embedded within these dominant 'social education' discourses are untroubled realist ontologies that aim to authenticize the "good citizen" through populist and humanist constructions. Stanley (1985) goes so far as to say that there may actually be agreement in the field of social education that is conservative in nature. Stanley (1985) states that "there may be a de facto consensus on a rationale for social education, as conservative cultural transmission to reify and reproduce the status quo of society and institutional arrangements" (p. 348). The effect of this consensus, is a reductionist Curriculum Space. However, Stanley (1992) presents a radical positionality that provides an other space for discussion of the possibilities for postmodernism and poststructuralism. Thus this constant call for the salvation of the "good citizen" (in multicultural education and teacher education, for example) may be interrogated using counterhegemonic discourses, which, according to Stanley, poststructuralism makes possible by highlighting the tensions of critical efforts in social education:

> What remains unclear in the debate within critical pedagogy is the relationship (or tension) between utopian thought, values, and pragmatic theory. In other words, while the postmodern and poststructuralist critique has led many radical educators to accept the problematic and contingent nature of all values—including those of radical democracy—there remains

an inclination on the part of critical educators to employ such contingent values (e.g., emancipation, freedom, empowerment, democracy, justice, solidarity, etc.) as the basis of a utopian view to orient sociocultural formation (Stanley, 1992, p. 172).

Stanley (1992) concludes with the caveat that poststructuralism is anti-foundational and thus helps to illuminate and radicalize the emancipatory potential of social education. According to Stanley, it is a way to "understand the 'textuality' of the social world in which we live and to act to change that world. In this sense, poststructuralism is not merely a method at the disposal of any political movement (a nihilistic position) but a way of understanding the human condition that is essential to counterhegemonic praxis" (p. 189). This is the aim of Curriculum Spaces as an approach to reveal how the textuality of the spaces of being are framed and thus provide ways to interrupt this reduction. Even emancipatory projects, such as the Charter School Movement, are embedded within social discourses that normalize. They produce tensions.

These tensions include the normalizing tendencies of mainstream culture and this suggests that even a critical perspective fails to disrupt or destabilize the populist foundations that continue to exclude and silence the "voices" of marginalized social groups and reduce subject positions to normalized and regulated identities. Popkewitz (1998c) concludes, "Thus, while we can applaud the new curriculum of inclusion as creating spaces for groups previously excluded, curriculum theory also needs to consider the inscription of norms that are embodied in the representational practices" (p. 98). Popkewitz's (1998c) analysis of the redemptive culture of the social and human sciences presents possibilities for a Foucauldian treatment of the field that allows us to work within the historically and politically situated field and against the normalizing tendencies of the dominant discourses in social education. According to Popkewitz, the influence of populism within scientific research has become manifest in assumptions that knowledge of the sciences can serve the democratic ideals of autonomy, empowerment and emancipation.

> The social sciences developed in a manner parallel to the state bureaucracy. The social sciences provided the disciplinary knowledge that linked new civil institutions with the liberal democratic political rationalities of the state. The construction of freedom became a problem of the social administration of the autonomous, self-motivated citizen (Popkewitz, 1998c, p. 3).

The Good Teacher

So, the best of intentions in the social sciences fall into spaces that struggle to serve democratic ideals while at the same time reproduce regimes of truth that exclude and reduce. Redemption in the name of democracy.

Social and Educational Discourses

Technologies of power and the embodiment of the redemptive culture of social scientific research are discussed by Popkewitz (1998a) as in danger of reinscribing historical exclusions and obscuring power relations in research. He suggests that institutional processes normalized and regulated individuals in order to produce docile bodies while concealing the relations of power that shaped the democratic project (Foucault, 1977; Popkewitz, 1998a). "My argument is that the particular ideas of progress and redemption inscribed in the social sciences are the effects of power which, when they go unnoticed in contemporary research and policy, may inter and enclose the possibility of change by reinscribing the very rules of reason and practice that need to be struggled against" (Popkewitz, 1998a, pp. 2–3).

Truth and power circulate throughout the system. The populist goals of social studies education, for example, are immersed within this system. Dominant conceptions of citizenship prescribed by particularist notions of democratic participation have created a totalizing and exclusivist ideology that serves to silence cultural differences. "While the redemptive theme is rhetorically positioned in the name of democratic principles, the concrete strategies are concerned with the governing of the soul. This reconstitutes the historical relation of the register of social administration and the register of freedom that tied the state and social sciences at the turn of the century" (Popkewitz, 1998a, p. 15).

Foucault (1991) interrogated the "governmentality" of the modern state and the administering of such dichotomies as freedom-civic competence and public-private and the self-regulation of modern institutions as "transformative institutions." I found this concept of governmentality to be a very useful concept when deconstructing the conditions by which the practices of collaboration and PDSs in social education, for example, are constructed as technologies of the modernist project.

This may suggest some reasons why education, both schooling and university sectors, has become so central in the development of new forms of governmentality, exemplifying new strategies, tactics and techniques of power to furnish what had become the major form of power relations defining institutions and individuals in Western societies. The institutions of formal education, schools and universities have become central to the 'disciplining' in most if not all other fields (Popkewitz and Brennan, 1998).

One way to sustain rigorous questioning of the "truth" embodied in educational work and research is to articulate and disrupt the "natural" (thus neutral) foundations of the dominant discourses (Popkewitz and Brennan, 1998). Truth, according to Foucault, is played out in the three-dimensional space of knowledge, subjectivity and power (Simola, Heikkinen, and Silvonen, 1998). This is an important point to consider when studying the dominant discourses in teacher education and multicultural education, as the "truth" of the field/area can be deconstructed—as can the ways in which the "subject"/the "good" citizen/the "good" student is constituted and constitutes him/herself. An investigation of the production of "truth" and the "subject" reveals the ways in which the field has excluded and silenced marginal discourses (Apple, 1996; Stanley, 1992; Lincoln, 1998; Popkewitz, 1998a).

Teacher Education Reform Rhetoric—The Professional Development School Model

As discussed in chapter two, one of my first research projects aimed to historicize the discourse practices that constructed the notion of "good teacher" in the PDS model as manifested at a large mid-west research institution (Cary, 1999b). This study highlighted the need for a more situated and complicated knowing of the assumptions framing concepts such as professional/expert knowledge, legitimate knowledge, and authentic/practical knowledge.

> If we think historically about the professional knowledge in teaching, there are three dimensions of historical interest here. They are (a) a view of progress in which change in society and the individual can be brought about through rational planning and social engineering; (b) a notion of the expert knowledge to provide that guidance; and (c) a populism, that is, a view that

the expert is in service of the democratic ideal (Popkewitz and Simola, 1996, p. 122).

The study focused on the PDS model that arose from the reform agenda of the Holmes Group (1986–1995). It triggered a plethora of unique cultures that highlight the limits of universalist assumptions and representations within colleges of education across the country. However, although successes and failures of the model have been well documented, critical research approaching the manifestation of the effects of power, the epistemological assumptions that frame the model and the textual discourses surrounding it have been lacking. Fullan et al. (1998) highlight the stalling of the reform effort as mired in the institutionalization of education and the resistance to change at this level. Yet, there is little analysis of the foundations of the reform effort and the assumptions that mire it in these very institutions. In this study I pursue the "stalling" of the PDS model as a call for an investigation of the foundational assumptions that frame it.

As stated previously, the study focused on the "center" of the PDS model manifested in a large mi-western research institution as socially constituted and historically produced through a critical analysis of the surrounding discourses, from societal to institutional and local (Cary, 1999). If we consider the ways in which total institutions produce regulated docile bodies of their inmates to create an efficient machine, how may this challenge the notion that schools (or universities) can "create" empowered and emancipated citizens?

Foundational Humanist Assumptions. In studying discourses of the PDS model, the foundational humanist assumptions of educational and social scientific research emerged as a skeletal organizational framework. The critical discourse analysis of interviews, official documents, educational reform literature, and critical research texts repeatedly highlighted a number of terms. Perfectibility, progress, professionalism, good teaching, realist ontologies of authenticity and practice, humanist and populist rhetoric, democratic ideals of citizenship (e.g., autonomy, empowerment and emancipation) and agency emerged. These terms were then used as a framework for the data analysis to both highlight the foundational assumptions of PDS and also investigate the utility of Popkewitz's (1998a) conceptualization of the culture of redemption in the PDS.

The foundational assumptions in the modernist knowledge project in the social and educational sciences discussed by Lincoln (1998) must be taken one step further to reveal the inscription of progress as a neutral central tenet (Popkewitz and Brennan, 1998). The efforts of the 1980s to reform schooling and professionalize teachers were framed by a number of foundational organizational assumptions that further "governed" the teacher's soul (or "subjectivity"). These assumptions included: issues of fragmentation of knowledge; further specialization and the sequential organization of knowledge; and the construction of possessive individualism and utilitarian thought that increased self-regulation as it deskilled teachers by decreasing teacher responsibility for curriculum decision-making. Moreover:

> The anomalies inherent in these reports [of the 1980s] are further exacerbated in that the reform efforts overlook the political and historical background of public schooling....The Holmes Group and Carnegie reports support their arguments by drawing on an idealized version of law and medicine. Altruistic ideals of professionals working for social betterment are portrayed, an approach that ignores the complex political, economic, and structural issues that underlie the cultural, social authority of professions. Whatever important social services are associated with professions, the publicly defined characteristics are myths that legitimate existing authority rather than illuminate the workings and contributions of the professions (Popkewitz, 1991, p. 161).

It has been suggested that these teacher education reforms reflect a nationalistic, masculinist vision assuming possessive individualism and efficiency of the market (a form of social efficiency revisited; see Labaree, 1995; Popkewitz, 1998c). According to Popkewitz (1998c), social administration was the foundational concept of schooling at the turn of the century that aimed to rescue the child so that he or she might become a self-disciplined, productive citizen. His analysis of constructivist pedagogy and educational reform efforts highlighted the way they are founded on the modernist theories of people like Dewey and Vygotsky linking the belief in scientific rationality with the potential of reason to produce social progress (Popkewitz, 1998d). Ultimately this was a form of governmentality, and the contemporary conceptualizations of pedagogy and teacher education reforms are still attempting to govern/rescue the souls of children and teachers at a time when individuality is less stable. "The professional teacher is self-governing and has greater local responsibility in implementing the curriculum decisions—a normativity also found in the structuring of the new constructivist teacher that, as discussed earlier, cites Dewey and Vygotsky as sources of its vision" (Popkewitz, 1998d, p. 553). This is neither inherently good nor bad, of course, just not to be taken as natural or unproblematic in any discussion about the social construction of knowledge.

Scientific Rationalism and Technical Competence. David Labaree (1992, 1995, 1996) outlined a number of issues in this area by focusing on the discourse of the Holmes Group reforms. He suggests that the way the discourse practices of the Holmes Group work to codify, develop and implement professional knowledge and the desire for the masculinization of the profession through the development of an objective, common body of knowledge based on the "superiority" of scientific claims, is a move away from the historically feminized profession (Labaree, 1992). This "expert knowledge" is a framework that positions technical knowledge as superior to political knowledge and validates this through the "science" of teaching. However, he concludes that this is an intellectually reduced notion of practice. His work is useful in suggesting/creating spaces from which to historicize the rhetoric of the professionalization reform movement from which the PDS model emerged. Throughout this work he has emphasized the scientific rationalist foundations for the reform movement that began with the Carnegie Task Force Report, *A Nation Prepared: Teachers for the 21st Century*, and the first Holmes Group Report, *Tomorrow's Teachers*. The desire (or object of desire) that emerges for the validation of the profession through the development of the "science of teaching," according to Labaree, was central to the move. The adapted medical school model, however, was mired in epistemological assumptions that increased the normalization of the profession and were based on the humanist foundations of public schooling in this country:

> According to this view, the creation of a professional teaching force will enable us to pursue more effectively all of the major social goals that Americans have traditionally assigned to public schools: social efficiency (raising the standard of living via enhanced skill training); social mobility (increasing social opportunity for the underclass); and political equality (enhancing students' ability to function in a democracy) (Labaree, 1992, p. 127).

Labaree (1992) highlights how embedded in this move toward professionalism was an emphasis on technical competence highlighted through the development of PDSs. The gendered nature of the goals of the reform movements, according to Labaree (1992), highlight the desire for increased status as a move away from the stereotypical "female" teacher role of nurturer and caregiver, to the technical competence of a common body of professional knowledge founded on masculinist assumptions of the superiority of scientific claims.

> Professionalization offers the teacher a way to escape identification with the unpaid and uncredentialed status of mother. The new professional teacher—especially a board-certified "lead" or "career professional" teacher—would be well paid and formally credentialed, with an education and a status within hailing distance of the high professions (Labaree, 1992, p. 132).

Call it "physics envy" (Lather, 1994), hard science, or high professions—the move indicated a shift away from situated knowing to the development of a common scientifically-based professional knowledge and masculinist technical competence. The notion of common professional knowledge and standards paradoxically presented in these reports, and the following Holmes Group Reports, were founded on notions of teacher autonomy, empowerment and merit. "Apparently, thinking of teaching's femaleness as unprofessional, the professionalizers seem to be trying to reshape the female schoolteacher in the image of the male physician" (Labaree, 1992, p. 133).

It is vital to note, however, that the paradigmatic assumptions of the scientific rationalist move were founded in an increasingly shaky and outmoded positivist paradigm that was being successfully challenged in the "hard sciences" (Harding, 1987). Along the same lines, Labaree (1992) suggested, "teacher educators may well be hitching their hopes to a research structure that is in the process of molting, which poses the possibility that they could be left behind clutching an empty shell" (p. 146). A tension thus exists between the progressivist notions of empowerment and excellence and the discourses that are embedded within this reform movement may be seen as enhancing "social inequality and educational hierarchy and thereby undermin[ing] the efforts to achieve progressivist ends" (p.

145), and as it drives for a politics of expert and male-dominated status within a formal rationalist environment.

Labaree (1992) highlights the way the subject construction of "good" teacher seems to be informed and shaped by masculinist and scientistic notions relying on the development of an "objective" body of scientific knowledge which in turn promotes criteria that enhance rationalization through the standardization of professional technical proficiency. This move focuses on "practice" and the superiority of technical competence. Conversely, this has subverted the focus from the political side of the profession/activity.

The continuing tensions between the social administration of the individual and freedom become manifest, therefore, in such reform efforts as the PDS. The assumed site of this struggle is often the normalized construction of the characteristics and capabilities of the "good" teacher. This is a dangerous assumption, according to Popkewitz (2000), and he goes on to call for increased scrutiny and interpretation of the ways in which the governing principles of reform talk are illustrative of the effects of power. This site is contested terrain, and historically the social institution of teacher education has become concerned with the production of knowledge submerged within universal and secularized moral values in the modern era (Popkewitz and Simola, 1996). This "modernization" of the governing practices of professionalization also relates to the systems of knowledge that produce the "good" (self-governed and autonomous) citizen:

> The taken-for-granted assumptions behind turn-of-the-century discourses about childhood, the state and schooling came from social engineering. It was assumed that proper planning would produce the New Citizen/'New Man' [sic] who could perform competently in the new social, economic, political and cultural contexts. The 'New Man' would be self-disciplined, self-motivated and 'reasonable' as a productive member of the new collective social projects of the day (Popkewitz and Simola, 1996, p. 14).

From the desire for a "professional," authentic teacher idealized through discourses reducing expert knowledge to masculinized, scientistic constructions, I highlight below a specific theme that emerged from the data of the study that suggests the spaces of knowing teachers are discursively produced at the societal level.

Analytical Moments in PDS. Throughout the analysis of the data the issues and paradoxes/problems of PDS emerged. Is this resistance? Britzman (1998) states that an insistence for immediate change may actually be a symptom of resistance: "People do not give up their libidinal positions easily, and when encountering differences, they seem to work hard to assert their own continuity" (p. 10), as the ego defends itself from what seems worrisome, dangerous and senseless. Change in teacher education, and then change within a PDS site (teachers come and go, faculty come and go) may make this experience seem dangerous and senseless. In the interviews some of the teachers 'invited' into the PDS stated that they felt they were being recruited for the PhD program (Loadman and Klecker, 1996) and this reflects one of the dangers of PDS, that is, the danger of constructing teachers as professional/unprofessional depending on their suitability for 'invitation' into a PDS. This issue emerged from the data as one of invitation. It was fascinating to see how who (the teachers in the field) gets invited and who dies (resigns, burns out, is no longer funded by the university) raises questions of the myth of neutrality surrounding participation in the PDS and highlights the conflict within. The interviews revealed that a framing assumption of the PDS was that not all teachers were cut out to be clinical educators (Chase and Merryfield 1998). What did this mean for rethinking PDS? Who gets invited, for example, and under what conditions? Professional development to what end? This highlights the possible and the impossible nature of professional development and demystifies inauthentic professional development (Anderson, 1998). This also suggests that PDS is a mastery project reflecting curative thoughts and desires (Britzman 1998). The elevating of practice over theory through the 'bridging' mechanisms of PDS highlights the danger of assuming theory and practice are statically framed within the university and schools, respectively.

I used the idea of an 'invitation' because it not only emerged from the data, but it was also an evocative idea from which to problematize the relatively uncomplicated discussions that often frame PDS. I used 'invitation' to frame my ethnographic moment of entry and also to double as the moment of mutual 'not knowing'/'seduction' by participants and the institution itself with/in the initial presentation of the ideas and promise of PDS. The following footnote from my textual analysis highlights this point:

It was something new and exciting for those 'invited' into the conversation. The source of the invitations and the 'origins' of the reform movement have not been researched beyond critical realist issues of power and authority. Labaree's work (1992), for example, talks of the rhetoric that frames the PDS but the data here highlight the fact that there was a 'not knowing' moment within this experience that could be translated into a dance of seduction with an initial desire to be involved in a 'better' type of teacher education.

Multiple reasons for responding to the initial invitation were given. For example, Maxine initially desired an invitation to the PDS because she wanted to bring together her established collaborative projects in teacher education with a mandated reform effort. Richard desired reform in schools and universities. The 'invitational' moment also brings to bear questions about who gets invited and the unwritten/invisible criteria for selection to this culture of reform. What makes a 'good' PDS teacher, professor, school site? It seemed as if the discursive practices of PDS legitimized the assumptions of progress and neutrality, while also regulating the experiences of individuals involved. Issues of invitations, membership, established relationships and PDS as an institutional technology of power were discussed. Who gets invited? How are they invited? How does this shape the discursive power relations within a PDS? Popkewitz's (1998c) concern with the redemptive nature of social and educational discourses in teacher education reform provided a vital insight into the study of PDS. It is fascinating, however, how the similar notions of good citizen, and in the next exemplar, good student, also occurs in school level reform. Curriculum spaces are discursively produced and shape the way we know reform, teachers and students at the societal level. This understanding leads us to the questions I framed on PDS and led me to the charter school reform effort.

The Charter School for 'Push-Out Recovery'

Studying the ways we know teachers, students and reform at the societal level in the Charter School Movement is another fertile site of study. I first entered the Charter School debate because I was interested in two vital questions—What about the students who get 'pushed-out' of school? What other spaces are there for students who have 'failed' in the system? (Pinar et al., 1995). This research project looked at an alternative education setting, a Charter School, described as a 'push-out recovery program' – a marginalized curriculum with a desire for community. The Charter School in central Texas—EdgeWorks (pseudonym)—was particularly interesting because it provided an educational space for individuals who chose this setting for a variety of reasons including histories of exclusion from public schools for a variety of complicated social and cultural reasons. McNeil (2000), Valenzuela (1999) and Popkewitz (1998a) discussed the various ways the discourses of schooling exclude and refuse to educate those 'outside' the mainstream, as a result of cultural, societal and socioeconomic factors. This study brought together my own work on two fronts: previous discussions of inclusion/exclusion and citizenship in social and educational discourses (Cary, 1999b; 2001) outlined earlier in this chapter; and, the study of young people who are excluded in their subject position of Outsiders, such as female juvenile offenders (Cary, 2003b), discussed in chapter four. Bringing these two areas together in this study allowed for the investigation of the factors of exclusion and the way the social and educational discourses play out in an 'alternative' setting.

My previous work had been more comfortably (if that is possible) postmodern. I determined that I needed to so something that 'made a difference.' This project fit both frames. It investigated exclusionary practices (and the redemptive foundation of educational reform) and also raised questions of how the negotiation of subject positions and knowledge production plays out in this arena.

> Charter Schools are an important site of study as they figure so prominently in current educational reform efforts as a response to the call for accountability. Before these unconventional public schools vaulted into the spotlight in the mid-1990's, education reform in the United States was nearing paralysis—stalemated by politics, confused by the cacophony of a thousand schemes working at cross-purposes, and hobbled by most people's inability to imagine anything very different from the schools they had attended decades earlier (Finn, Manno and Vanourek, 2000, p. 13).

It was an ethnographic study conducted over approximately twelve months at the Charter School. This involved an immersion in the 'culture' of the school through extended hours of observation. I visited classrooms and met the administrators, teachers and students. Data sources included observations, interviews (students, teachers and administrators) and researcher journal as well as the collection of documents from the school and educational environment (government educational policy documents, school policy/goals and mission statement such as a web site). The Charter School provided educational services for young people 16–20 who aimed to receive their General Equivalency Diploma (GED) and/or their high school certificate and there are 4 administrators, 16 teachers and between 250–300 students. I used both random sampling (hallway interactions, classroom discussions, student volunteers) and purposeful sampling (specifically targeting the administrators and teachers) and snowball sampling (interviewing teachers and students recommended by other participants). However, as the project went on I began to focus mainly on the students and their perceptions of the charter school experience.

It is vital to situate this study in the light of the national, and state, mandated educational reforms.

> Judged by the numbers alone, the charter movement is a force to be reckoned with. What's more, it is clearer than ever that charters are compatible with other important school reforms underway in the United States: with 'standards-based' reform and its approach to accountability (which is the focus of a lively debate catalyzed by President Bush's proposals to transform federal education policy); with the intensifying focus on school results rather than inputs; with the effort to offer families more choices among more diverse schools; with the trend toward contracting and outsourcing education services and school makeovers; with the diversity and feisty independence of the growing home school movement; with the impulse to provide more small schools for children for reasons of both education and safety; and with accelerating change on the technology front (Finn et al., 2000, p. xii).

Discursively Produced Spaces of Knowing. It became clear to me after extensive analysis and struggling with the data/discourses that *my way of knowing* the charter school was framed or produced by discourses of failure or crisis. The students, on the other hand, *knew* the charter school as full of success, hope and possibility. Their way of knowing interrupted my position and led to the understanding that the discursive production of Curriculum Spaces provides insight into the way we know what we know and moves educational research into a new space or place. Otherwise, it all falls into the hole of difference—one which reduces and demeans the experience and one which highlights the static nature of discussions of epistemology as an individual raced, gendered, classed or sexualized theory of knowledge. This removes the process of knowing from the equation; thus it becomes a confessional moment or a claim to the authentic authorial analysis. As Villenas (1996) reminds us, we are all colonizers in our role as academic researchers.

However, the interesting part of this study is in two areas: (1) my 'knowing' of the Charter School and, (2) the students 'knowing' of the Charter School. First, a number of discourses emerged within my frame of knowing that I realized well into the project had shaped not only my choice of topic, but also the questions I was asking about exclusion and the experience of the charter school as a redemptive institution. These discourses affected my methodology decision (an ethnographic study), the choice of setting and the choice of data sources, data collection methods and analytical tools. However, it is in the final analysis, bringing together the framing literature and studying the discourses using the postmodern literature outlined in the Curriculum Spaces Research Theory, that I found the following discourses that shaped my knowing. This is a vital move, often missed in novice educational research. It is the final step—bringing it all together, beyond positionality, beyond methodology and beyond realist descriptions that avoid responsibility and deeper analysis.

The discourses of failure that shaped my knowing included the notions of the failure of social justice and equity in the public school system and the way national, and state, level legislation and mandated educational reforms situate the schools, students and teachers of this nation as in crisis. I also knew the charter school through a critical analysis of the Charter School Reform Movement which frames public schools as failing and focuses the need for more choice which the rhetoric suggests, is aimed at helping 'disadvantaged students'(Finn et al., 2000). This study occurred during the debate on 'science' that reflects current moves in educational research and the call for more replicable and consumable research and reinscribing limited notions of research (St. Pierre, 2002; Berliner, 2002; Erickson and Gutierrez, 2002). Indeed, my own research history focused on exclusion and crisis, for example, on the gendered and raced social construction of citizenship in teacher education and 'bad' girls as citizen outcasts in the Juvenile Justice System (Cary, 2001; Cary, 2003b). Finally, the fixed signification of 'drop-outs' that the charter school resists and redefines from a critical perspective, thus calling itself a 'push-out recovery program,' fit with my critical lens and supported my interest in the 'push-out' stories that emerged in the following discussion of the students' emergent Curriculum Spaces. However, it also highlighted that the students

The Good Teacher

resisted or refused this exclusion approach. They were much more interested in the future.

Second, the way the students knew the charter school interrupted my privileged position. It was the students' refusal of my own constructed curriculum spaces that revealed the importance of this 'final-step' analysis made possible by the Curriculum Spaces Research Theory. A number of discourses emerged from the student interviews. I had conducted an ethnographic study of the charter school but it was the student data that became the central focus of the study. The students knew themselves through discourses of success, hope and possibility. During the interviews they constantly moved into discussions of the future and, in many cases, this was the first time in their educational experiences they saw themselves as successful. The discourses of success included the need for respect and help from the teachers and administrators. This was highlighted in every interview. It was so important that one student was on the verge of dropping out when she overheard some teachers 'dissing' the students. It was clearly a fragile sense of respect and help that emerged in contrast to the experiences in the public school system. According to the students judging the students was one of the biggest failures of the teachers in the public school system. The second major discourse that emerged was leadership. In the interviews the students all mentioned a variety of opportunities and experiences that framed them as leaders and they knew this space very differently than previous spaces of knowing. Next was a discourse of future possibilities. This included jobs, careers and further study at the community college and university. Success in learning was another framing discourse that highlighted the different Curriculum Space of knowing that framed the students in the study. Community was a vital discourse that connected the students in the charter school. They recognized each other. According to one administrator, they were the 10% most marginalized students (for a variety of reasons) from the public schools that found their way to the charter school. It was described by one of the students as a 'ghetto school'—not in a negative sense but in the way it was home to previously excluded and disenfranchised youth. It was not really a 'school,' in the way they knew schools.

For example, I observed a history and government class once a week for a semester. I was constantly uncomfortable—many of my own notions of good teaching were not reflected in the environment.

And yet, it seemed that many of the students were succeeding (passing tests—passing the class—getting the GED or High School Diploma). It reminded me of the way I know teaching and the way I was knowing/interpreting the Edgeworks classroom was a construction of a number of discourses that I had internalized through my eighteen years of teaching experience.

> Students are late to class—Jose—confronted a little bit by DJ—storms out and stating he might as well go and eat and not come at all (Notes from Observation—052303).

According to one administrator, the charter school population was not representative of a 'normal' school:

> I always thought that in a traditional school you have 10% of the population that doesn't come to school, that may dress different, that may use drugs more frequently than the other groups, or they may be just lost in this setting—I would say 85% of our population is that 10% (Samantha, Counselor/administrator).

The students talked a lot about the violence at the charter school and the shared experiences of activities that have led them to this place.

> Margot: Actually, I think there's more violence [here].
> L: Interesting. So how's it different from the public schools?
> Margot: I have to, I love Edgeworks but it's a really ghetto school. Because no-one really knows about it except, you know, people that drop out, and like mothers that are teenagers, and stuff. So, you know, not that many upper class people come here, just because they probably don't know about it yet. I don't think that they would have problems.

Margot continued on the difference of the Charter School from other schools:

> Margot: There is a lot of energy. Too much energy, sometimes. But, I mean, it's just like, we know where we've been. Like, we know everybody's story, because it's our own story. Some may be more tragic than others, but we still know where they're coming from.

However, the majority of the students stated that they had enrolled at Edgeworks because they saw a chance to succeed. The students entered a Curriculum Space of possibility and redemption. They were seen as 'redeemable.' It is not a surprise nor a condemnation that we hope for redemption through schooling (Popkewitz, 1998c). It was a strong discourse of this setting and after multiple positive

The Good Teacher

experiences in this new space the students talked about being 'ambassadors' for the school, being seen as leaders, and receiving awards.

> Margot: Actually, yea. I was at the bottom of my school when I went to Westhills. Now, I'm a student ambassador for this school. So, I've moved that far up. My confidence has gone that far up that, you know, I feel like I can conquer the world.

And:

> Alex: I do computers, and the men, I mean the people I work for, they sent me to Washington, DC.
> L: So what did you do in Washington, DC?
> Alex: We went to Capitol Hill and we talked to the Congressmen, trying to get funding for the program and I, we, did pretty good up there....
> Alex: Yea, flew up there. They paid for the ticket and everything. And if they'll just give me the opportunity to do things and chances, and let me do things I can do.

My original intention was to reveal the discourses of exclusion that shaped the students' educational lives and framed the redemptive mission of the school. However, the discourses outlined above far outweighed the power of the exclusion discourses. The student data did contain discourses of exclusion, but from a different position. The students knew these discourses from a distance. It seemed to be a protective distance that resulted from histories of marginalization—but it also translated as outside of their control and was not framed as a discourse of failure. The majority of the students dismissed issues of responsibility or involvement, highlighting their awareness of systemic failures, not personal failure. It was a very powerful move, similar to the findings encountered by DeCuir and Dixson (2004). Only two of the students mentioned bad choices or knew the charter school as a "last chance." The majority did not mention responsibility. Rather, they presented the systemic and structural failures of the public school system with great insight. However, the discourse that really affected them the most, as mentioned earlier, was the issue of being judged. The majority of the students had stories of being judged and stereotyped in their previous educational experiences. It seemed this was the most damaging discourse.

> Margot: Oh yes. I don't know why, but, I guess, Westhills, just like, they didn't really care. And they were, you know like, once I did something bad, they thought that I was a bad kid forever. And it was just like that one time, so I actually started

thinking "oh, I'm never going to be able to graduate. Why am I even here?" So that's what happened.

A.J.: At Smith I felt like I couldn't even get permission to go to the bathroom. I couldn't do this but a white girl asks, "oh can I go to the restroom?" She said, "yea, just let me get you a pass". I ask and "No, you can't go to the bathroom. You've got to wait to go downstairs." I just didn't like it. And I called a few teachers on it and stuff, and they're like "you're crazy, no I'm not into that, whatever." I'm like "well, then how come she gets to go to the bathroom?" "Because ????. Okay, I've got to go to the bathroom. So, I walk out and then I called my Dad, because they were making a big thing out of something small. I just, I just didn't like.

Redemptive Cultures

Popkewitz (1998c) addressed the historical foundations of the social and educational sciences and described the redemptive culture that arose from populist goals which inscribed democratic ideals within the study of the social sciences. Autonomy, empowerment, and emancipation were promised—yet the institutional processes normalized and regulated individuals to produce docile bodies instead. This occurred through self-regulation and surveillance that were concealed in relations of power shaped with/in the democratic project (Popkewitz, 1998c; Foucault, 1977). According to Popkewitz (1998c), the development of the social sciences paralleled state bureaucracy. "The social sciences provided the disciplinary knowledge that linked new civil institutions with the liberal democratic political rationalities of the state. The construction of freedom became a problem of the social administration of the autonomous, self-motivated citizen" (Popkewitz, 1998c, p. 3).

By highlighting the culture of redemption that emerged within the social sciences, Popkewitz (1998a) suggests that it is possible to work within and against the governing practices that disqualify certain groups from participation, thus interrupting the normalizing tendencies of the total institution of education.

> The idea that the state could administer human freedom involved social planning. The new citizen—or "new man," a term that circulated into the early 20th century—connected the scope and aspirations of public powers with the personal and subjective capacities of individuals. New institutions of health, employment, and education tied the new social welfare goals of the state with a particular form of scientific expertise that was to organize subjectivities. That is, the way in which individuals personally experienced and understood the self and the world related to social practices and power

The Good Teacher

relations which constituted the order through which meaning was structured (see, e.g., Scott, 1991). A complex apparatus of institutions, for example, targeted the child, the family, the worker, and the new citizen. Policy and science were to produce a mentality by which the new citizen or individual acted and participated in what Michel Foucault (1979b) called 'governmentality' (Popkewitz, 1998a, p. 4).

Even the progressive pragmatism of John Dewey when seen in this light is indicative of the universal modernist project to create productive and worthwhile citizens through populist rhetoric that inscribed specific "dominant" rules of participation (Lincoln, 1998; Popkewitz, 1991, 1998d). Thus, the redemptive culture of populist rhetoric in teacher education governed the souls of individual students and teachers to work for the "greater good" within certain boundaries.

While the current rhetoric is about giving voice to excluded groups and therefore being democratic and emancipatory, this frequent call to reconstitute principles of participation and responsibility occurs through redemptive discourses that are to discipline parents and the community in saving the child. That call for salvation entails discourses that construct particular sets of norms about the child, parent and community that emerge from political rationalities about populations of targeted groups. It is not some 'natural' parent or community that participates, but groups defined through the ordering, normalizing and dividing practices inscribed in the discourses of participation (Popkewitz, 1998a, p. 11).

Social education discourses, as discussed here, provide an avenue for rethinking the ways in which knowledge and power intersect in higher education and frame the way we know reform. It is vital to create a place from which to interrogate the exclusivity of hegemonic discourses (Popkewitz, 1998a; Lincoln, 1998). "Higher education is the only organization we have which is dedicated first and foremost to the generation of new knowledge, and the re-consideration, reconstruction, revision, and reshaping of received knowledge" (Lincoln, 1998, p. 12). Both teacher education and multicultural education may be seen as redemptive projects. They both aim to provide multiple opportunities for the development of more egalitarian schools and social transformation in general (Goodman, 1995). I continue to question the claims to innocence of this conceptualization through using the Curriculum Spaces Research Theory lens. In this way we can study the discourses that frame the way we know these movements and how we make curriculum decisions about teacher education and charter schools. I continue to wonder about the masculinist, scientific, technical rationalist conceptualization of "teacher" in the reform talk and the dangers of reducing students to subjects to be saved and made into good citizens in the Charter School movement. Understanding the discursive production of such Curriculum Spaces at the societal level is one way of beginning the interruption of exclusivist practices and curriculum decision-making that often occurs without this level of reflection.

4
Gender and Race: Discourses That Other

From the societal level, we now move into the institutional discourses and spaces of knowing in education. While it is vital to note the separation of the discursive production of knowing into three levels (societal, institutional and local, according to Fairclough, 1995) is artificial, problematic and structuralist—it is also useful. Thus, it is the guiding frame for the first part of this book. Chapter two presented exemplars of the Curriculum Spaces Research Theory at the societal level. In this chapter, two exemplars are presented in order to address how race and gender are embedded in certain educational discourses at institutional levels. Chapter five presents a more personal/ professional journey through the study of Curriculum Spaces. However, in this chapter the subject position of 'juvie girls' and the ways this subject position is made possible and impossible by the intersection of historical, social and cultural discourses is presented (Cary, 2003b). Following that, I present a brief discussion of the way multicultural education discourses have Whitened the debate about good education even with the best of intentions toward diversity (Cary, 2001). Finally, this chapter suggests that efforts to 'improve' the profession and address equity remain embedded within assumptions that normalize, and exclude, through race and gender.

Constructing Gender

> Girls are the fastest growing segment of the juvenile justice population, despite the overall drop in juvenile crime (*Justice by Gender: The lack of appropriate prevention, diversion and treatment alternatives for girls in the justice system.* 2001, p. 1).

As discussed earlier, the current Populist crisis concerning youth and violence has grave consequences for the lives of those labeled deviant, such as 'dropouts' and 'juvenile offenders.' In order to better understand and interrupt this crisis, I believe it is vital to consider the construction of gender and the construction of social total institutions (schools and institutions of detention) as historically framed through the intersections of multiple discursive practices. This chapter presents a journey toward a more adequate knowing of the ways gender and race play out in educational settings. In this case, the subjects are constructed as bad and pathologized as deviant in the discourses that frame female juvenile offenders in the United States. I came to this work as an experienced teacher and researcher with specific interests in the reductive epistemological spaces of girls in schools and the exclusivist nature of the redemptive public education project (Popkewitz, 1998c). This work draws upon two analytical methodologies—critical discourse analysis and deviant historiography of the Curriculum Spaces made im/possible by/for/with female juvenile offenders. The construction of 'good girl,' citizen, child, adolescence, aggression, social institutions of education and detention, Progressivist notions of woman (social hygienists and eugenicists), populist discourses—all these tie into a multiply layered discursive space that is exclusivist and reductive. It is by revealing some of the layers of discourse, I suggest, that we might complicate research concerning female juvenile offenders. Therefore, it is also vital that we then interrupt the normalizing framing assumptions of the public education project and the reductive practices of social institutions by deconstructing current research rhetoric and the im/possibility of 'giving voice' to excluded groups within total social institutions that continue to discipline and regulate (Popkewitz, 1998c, p. 11).

This interruption is important as it highlights the ways the framing assumptions continue to frame the 'participants' in such research as 'deviant' (Terry, 1991). In this way I aim to trouble the claim of innocence of those researchers immersed in redemptive practices that fail to investigate the epistemological assumptions (the im/possible spaces of being) that frame 'deviant' Others and thus reinscribe normalizing practices. Some of the framing historical discourses (regimes of truth) discussed here will include: the notion of deviant subjectivity; unhomelyness as a social construct; sexual deviance, gender and masculinizing discourses; parental control and patriarchy; and systemic/institutional technologies of power. From the construction of female aggression as deviant to the sexualizing of female behavior through historic moral projects and gynecological examinations of inmates, this study found that the framing discourses emerging from the research analyzed continued to suggest a central theme of deviant behavior. This was situated within a societal construct that highlights the im/possibility of socially acceptable female deviant or aggressive behavior and the reductive nature of gendered social roles.

Playing with the powerful work of Bhabha (1994), Visweswaran (1994), Dubois (1995) and Kaplan (1996), I have theorized this im/possible epistemological space as another way of looking at the concept of home and thus homelessness. This interrogation of 'home' is then linked with the idea of the normalizing and exclusive practices of total institutions and thus suggests that 'home' is an im/possibility for those constructed as deviant. However, what is most useful is the way Bhabha (1994) presents the possibility of going 'beyond' establishing boundaries, thus framing unhomeliness as a condition of a sense of relocation for those outside/marginalized from normalizing institutions. This unhomely space is not without home, nor homeless, but it also cannot be comfortably or easily accommodated into familiar divisions of social life (Bhabha, 1994).

I think this is useful to consider for the female juvenile offenders because Bhabha (1994) uses the concept of the unhomely space as a vital site for feminist resistance against the patriarchal and gendered nature of social reality by interrogating the domestic space as normalizing and the personal/public binary as regulatory. Bhabha moves beyond romantic notions of home by developing the concept of the unhomed/unhomely to create a space for cultural difference. "The unhomely moment relates to the traumatic ambivalences of a personal, psychic history to the wider disjunctions of political existence" (Bhabha, 1994, p. 11). In this way we may move beyond the notion of home to the space of the 'unhomely' and thus highlight the failure of the 'system' to provide homes for the juvenile offenders. Thus the dissonant even dissident histories and voices of women, the colonized, minority groups, and the bearers of policed sexualities may emerge (Bhabha, 1994). This suggests a space to redefine home and other total institutions in complicated and hopeful ways.

A Foucauldian analysis of the practices that govern the souls of female juvenile offenders, discussed earlier, is another way of highlighting the ways universalist assumptions reify an exclusive notion of a 'good citizen' or 'good girl' (Foucault, 1977). When we add this to the mix it also allows us to move beyond critical perspectives and encourages an increasing awareness of the technologies of power (the way power circulates) in the creation and production of the official (legitimate) knowledges and subjects—such as in institutions of detention/remand. Therefore, it begs the questions: What are the framing discourses around/about female juvenile offenders? How do these discourses frame the subject as deviant and thus unhomely?

Critical Discourse Analysis and Deviant Historiography

> The picture of the troubled girl in the juvenile justice system is beginning to emerge (*Justice by Gender*, 2001, p. 4).

Jennifer Terry's (1991) work on theorizing deviant historiography focused on the construction of deviant subjectivity with lesbians and gays. Her work is useful for this project because it highlights how studying historical texts and the emergent discourses might shed light on the deviant subject positions constructed or/for/with female juvenile offenders. Terry suggests a method for mapping the discursive and textual operations that are "at play in the historical emergence of subjects" (p. 55). Merging this method together with the work of Norman Fairclough (1995) on critical discourse analysis, as discussed previously, I am telling a story of the im/possibility of 'homing' those occupying the deviant subject position of the juvenile female offender. Fairclough highlights the multiple layers of text that reflect/reinscribe the discursive practices wandering through contextual, institutional and societal spaces of being.

The ways in which the female juvenile offenders have been constructed as deviant in these epistemological spaces includes the highly sexualized and pathologized medico-scientific discourses and the suggestion of masculine tendencies (aggression being a masculine construct). In the pages that follow I highlight the various 'events' of the story that has emerged over time and have structured the marginality of those marked as Other (Terry, 1991). Terry draws upon the work of Foucault, Deleuze and Spivak to suggest we read against the grain of the dominant histories that are often pejorative and oppressive for marginalized deviant subjects (Terry, 1991, p. 57).

This work is an attempt to analyze previously obscured or disconnected discourses that frame the construction of those we label 'female juvenile offenders'. Historical movements based on Progressive ideologies, the gendered construction of legal classifications and the very nature of aggression all suggest this is a very complicated space. The embodiment of the female juvenile offender as highly sexualized and the resultant pathological and psychiatric interpretations of behavior are major contributors to the

Gender and Race

powerful construction of this deviant subject position. From theorizing about the deficiency of the girls as unattractive and masculine in their behavior to suggesting that they were suffering from premenstrual syndrome (PMS), uninterrogated assumptions are dangerously reducing the possibility of 'homing' (providing homes for) these girls. The next section highlights the discourses and regimes of truth that emerged from the critical discourse analysis of the research on female juvenile offenders.

Constructing Discourses of the Deviant Female Juvenile Offender

> Young girls facing family fragmentation, victimization and abuse, serious physical and mental health disorders, school failure and conflicted relationships need the help of their communities to move beyond their chaotic histories and enable them to succeed (*Justice by Gender*, 2001, p. 8).

Parental control, institutional failure (or total institution exclusions) and the construction of deviant subjectivities all play a part here. The prevailing story in the populist media is that teens in America are out of control. In response to this crisis, government agencies must be given authority to control teens, otherwise society as we know it will be destroyed! (Michaelis, 1999). This crisis shows how these historic and contemporary discourses intersect and blur together to frame female juvenile offenders as deviant and unhomely individuals. These framing assumptions are embedded in the way we know, judge, convict and counsel young women. It would be of benefit to conduct further study on this topic and the ways in which it is reinforced in school settings, institutions of detention and even parental homes. Are 'bad girls' more problematic than 'bad boys'? The literature suggests that we deal with boys differently and in a way less harshly. From the gendered nature of the Juvenile Justice System and status offenses to the regulation of the female body, the intersecting discourses discussed here suggest that female juvenile offenders occupy a very complex and reductive deviant subject position.

Crisis Talk. One of the most significant discourses is reflected in the 'crisis talk' in populist forums such as the media and legislative agendas. The crisis affecting female juvenile offenders and thus threatening 'society' has been framed as an epidemic of violence of epic proportions (Michaelis, 1999; Rodriguez, 1997; Acland, 1995). In this section I will outline the work of a number of scholars who have written in response to or concerning this 'crisis'. For example, Acland (1995) refers to the crisis from a cultural studies perspective as a time of fear and instability that calls for increased surveillance and discipline that provides space for neoconservative responses. Within the same space of crisis talk and the construction of youth as violent and dangerous, Rodriguez (1997) wonders about the criminalization of youth as a contributing discourse. He states:

> What to do with those whom society cannot accommodate? Criminalize them. Outlaw their actions and creations. Declare them the enemy, then wage war. Emphasize the differences, the shade of skin, the accent in the speech or manner of clothes. Like the scapegoat of the Bible, place society's ills on them, then 'stone' them in absolution. It's convenient. It's logical. It doesn't work (Rodriguez, 1997, p. 250).

An extensive search of the research suggests that framing youth as violent and a threat to society is one of the most hotly debated and misunderstood issues in the United States. On this topic, Katz (1997) also refers to this regime of truth, when she says that the search for causes and explanations are a direct response to the media's claim of a national social and educational crisis. However, it is worth noting that Katz (1997) goes on to suggest that schools actually promote violence through the role of teachers and the structure of schools.

If we study this using the work of Popkewitz (1998c) and Terry (1991) and question how the redemptive nature of the educational and social sciences normalize deviant 'citizens,' then the work of Luis Rodriguez (1997) is a fascinating connection between populist crisis talk and the nature of society. Rodriguez (1997) refers to an article in the Chicago Tribune in May 1997 by Michael Doming. According to this article, a politician stated that the young should no longer be viewed as more redeemable than adults. However, Rodriguez responds by highlighting the ways in which schools, law enforcement, youth agencies and child protective services are faced with policies and directives to 'give up' on a significant section of young people. He calls for a national debate and challenges the populist notions and the exclusivist nature of crisis talk:

> It is time we challenged the concepts that young people are unredeemable, that 'superpredators' are prepared to overrun our streets in a generation or two, and that the only way to be safe is to build more prisons, institute 'zero

tolerance' wherever youth encounter programs and take the 'deviants' from our midst (Rodriguez, 1997, p. 7).

Philosophical Discourses. A number of studies analyzed focused on the deviant sociohistorical facts of female juvenile offenders in the United States and presented descriptively realist tales (Van Maanen, 1988). In this way the texts are univocal and offer only one reading so that the reader may cull the facts to support the 'correct' reading. The work of Acland (1995), Chesney-Lind (1989), Odem and Schlossman (1991), and Steet (1999) highlight the discursive practices surrounding the construction of the normalized subject position of woman and 'good' girl and thus the deviance of the Other. Beginning in the nineteenth century and shaping the institutional reforms and practices of the twentieth century was a focus on child-saving, eugenicism and social hygiene. The campaigns of the Eugenicists and Social Hygienists movements were highly influential in heightening public anxiety about the deviance of working-class female youth and their sexual activity during the Progressive Era and into the twenthieth century (Odem and Schlossman, 1991). The so-called 'illicit sexual activity' of female youth was constructed as a medical, biological and moral threat to society, according to civic leaders of this period. The Eugenicists identified the 'sex delinquent' as a major threat to the genetic purity of the population and thus threatened to 'propagate' individuals that could be mentally or biologically inferior. Thus "young female 'sex delinquents' became a prime object of the eugenicists' most prominent policy instrument—sterilization—a procedure that was implemented more widely in California than in any other state. . ." (Odem and Schlossman, 1991, p. 188). Also influential at this time were the Social Hygienists. They saw the 'sex delinquent' as a threat to society through the spread of venereal disease, as well as through the propagation of defective children. According to Odem and Schlossman (1991), this perspective was 'informed' by new discoveries regarding the pathology of syphilis and gonorrhea that resulted in national campaigns focusing on 'immoral' women and calling for compulsory testing and detention of prostitutes and young female offenders.

The Childsaving Movement was another extremely influential historic group. They attributed to a discourse that reflected notions of the 'child,' the 'good girl' and social redemption. "Indeed, work on the early history of the separate system for youth, reveals that concerns about girls' immoral conduct were really at the center of what some have called the 'childsaving movement' (Platt, 1969) that set up the juvenile system" (Chesney-Lind, 1989, p. 14). According to Chesney-Lind (1989), the Progressive era movements intended to establish separate institutions for youth and were 'keenly concerned' with the 'social ills' of prostitution and white slavery. However, the Childsaving Movement (led predominantly by women) was also a strong 'celebration' of women's domesticity that involved monitoring the behavior of young girls to prevent them from straying from the 'moral path' (Chesney-Lind, 1989). Thus, normalizing constructs such as self-regulation, 'publicly acceptable behavior' and the desired salvation of 'bad girls' emerged and were later reinscribed through these historic philosophical movements. According to Odem and Schlossman (1991), this led to civic leaders and court officials in the first two decades of the twentieth century to introducing innovative measures to control and rehabilitate delinquent girls as a response to the newly defined problem of the female 'sex delinquent' (with its attendant medical and biological dangers), such as harsher penalties and increased detention in juvenile facilities.

This movement also reflected the emergence of a new conceptualization of the period between child and adult. According to Acland (1995), we moved from an assumption of the innocence of children to the essential guilt of youth. Steet (1999) also addresses this move when she refers to the work of John Dewey and Jane Addams. According to Steet, these early reformers romantically reconstructed a preindustrial past using the sociocultural construction of innocent children being led to their 'appropriate places' in the adult world. She goes on to reference the way the politically conservative socially prominent middle class women who were in the Childsaving Movement reinforced a particular code of moral values. This code was threatened by immigrant, urban, industrial life/cultures. Embedded within these progressive representations, however, were patronizing, essentialist and reductionist notions of woman—well-intentioned, romantic, sincere, do-gooders.

The most important aspect of this historic discourse for contemporary female juvenile offenders is that aspects of such reductive and romantic notions of 'woman' continue to regulate female behavior today through the regimes of truth shaping the social institutions of the school, family and the legal system. So, not only is the 'deviant' girl unhomely, she is also unwomanly. Thus, the violence of the normalizing institutions on her body and the im/possibility of her space of being are more pronounced and the research to 'save' her and reform the institutions are embedded in such sociohistorical discourses of truth.

Sexual Deviance and Parental Control. Throughout the gendered constructions of the female juvenile offenders is the discourse on deviant (indeed rampant) sexuality. Chesney-Lind (1989) highlights the technologies of power in the total institutions that framed the girls as deviant and unhomely. As such female juvenile offenders have, according to a number of sources, often received more sanctions than their male counterparts in efforts to control them and regulate their 'unacceptable aggressive behavior' (Chesney-Lind, 1989; Odem and Schlossman, 1991; Chesney-Lind and Brown, 1999). Chesney-Lind (1989) suggests that girls were sanctioned/sentenced much more severely and that girls were twice as likely to be institutionalized. Upon institutionalization the girls also became subject to a process of physical examinations and regulation. This process reflected a pathological perspective on gender and female sexuality through a technology of power. In the period between 1920 and 1950 in Los Angeles all young women and girls sent to Juvenile Hall faced a pelvic examination and tested for venereal disease. If they were judged to be sexually active they were segregated from the others to prevent 'moral corruption' (Odem and Schlossman, 1991, p. 192).

Chesney-Lind (1989) explained that youthful female misbehavior was traditionally subject to surveillance for evidence of sexual 'misconduct' and institutions ensured that there was no contact with males as they set out to engage them in domestic pursuits and hold the girls until they were of marriageable age. This reduced the female juvenile offender to a highly sexualized and morally dangerous being. Institutional practices highlighted the body and sexual behavior of these girls in ways their male counterparts were not subject to. Once in the system court personnel further 'sexualized' virtually all female defiance and ignored other misbehavior (Chesney-Lind, 1989). A majority (90%) of the 220 girls charged in 1920 in Los Angeles were charged with offenses involving sexual behavior (Odem and Schlossman, 1991). This historic discourse sexualizing female juvenile offenders is reflected in the contemporary sexualization of female deviance as criminal activities by girls were historically overlooked so long as they did not appear to resist the accepted 'moral standards' of the day or the signal defiance of parental control (Chesney-Lind, 1989). Odem and Schlossman (1991) draw upon the work of Meda Chesney-Lind and thus highlight that the sexualization of female juvenile offenders in 1950 reflects the mindset and policy inventions of the Progressive Era and continued to dominate the practice of female juvenile justice even up to the dawn of the modern women's movement. Issues of deviancy permeate the realities constructed historically around female juvenile offenders and intersects with the gendered construction of delinquency. Although girls accounted for about 25% of all arrests of youth in the United States in 1994, delinquency was still considered a male domain (Chesney-Lind and Brown, 1999, citing the Federal Bureau of Investigation, 1995). Therefore, when girls and young women are discussed, the framing construction is about their 'dangerous' sexuality. Sexuality has thus been the organizing context discussions of the involvement of young women in the Juvenile Justice System (Chesney-Lind and Brown, 1999).

This brings us to another fascinating framing and shaping discursive practice—the role of parental control and patriarchy. In some ways this framing discourses of truth reflects the most common notion of 'home. Thus it is most powerful to consider the im/possibility of 'homing' female juvenile offenders in social institutions when one considers that, according to Chesney-Lind (1989), 'reporting' young women to the juvenile court system was most often initiated by parents and guardians. Parents most often reported their daughters as 'out of control.' "It has long been understood that a major reason for girls' presence in juvenile courts was the fact that their parents insisted on their arrest" (Chesney-Lind, 1989, p. 20). It is suggested that this pattern has historically maintained patriarchy and that efforts to 'protect' youth may also curb the right of young women to defy patriarchy (Chesney-Lind, 1989). Therefore, girls 'delinquent' behavior in gangs, for example, depicts them as "either tomboys or sex objects" (Chesney-Lind and Brown , 1999, p. 173). Conventional theorizing about juvenile delinquency thus continues to view girls' delinquency as deviant, interpersonal and sexual, yet boys' delinquent behavior is conceptualized as basically more serious, aggressive, and criminal. However, according to Chesney-Lind and Brown (1999), this view has been challenged by the large increases in arrests of women and girls during the 1960s and 1970s and the shift was attributed by many,

Gender and Race   89

(without the support of solid research) to the women's movement and the subsequent erosion of normative gender roles. Chesney-Lind (1989) suggests that official actions and reactions are major forces in women's oppression: "they have historically served to reinforce the obedience of all young women to the demands of patriarchal authority no matter how abusive and arbitrary" (p. 5). This then serves to reinforce and reinscribe the regimes of truth through oppressive discursive practices and punitive responses to female deviance.

Masculinizing and Engendering. Framing female juvenile offenders as highly sexualized deviant subjects is further exacerbated when constructed through dominant masculinized notions of aggression and delinquency. This tensions suggests the girls inhabiting the subject position are not only 'bad girls' but not 'girl-like' at all and the institutional responses fail to interrupt these constructions and thus make 'homing' them relatively impossible. This is because embedded within discussions of deviant behavior and delinquency are the limitations of correctional programs for female inmates (Adler, 1975). The conventional wisdom about incarcerating women does not reflect the changing role of women in American society. Adler (1975) suggested that a new genre of female offenders had been created. It was traditionally believed that imprisoned men were very dangerous but that imprisoned women were docile. Thus, the women and young girls who interrupt this historic construction do not subscribe to established/legitimate role distinctions as constructed through regimes of truth. Therefore, they continue to challenge both society and the corrections system to deal with them on equal terms (Adler, 1975). In contemporary settings female inmates have resisted incarceration through riots and escape, just as their male counterparts have. Thus they are no longer held to be passive, docile victims of 'victimless sexual and moral crimes'—indeed they are now more dangerous— even more unwomanly. Thus the "applecart of benign neglect which has ruled the field of female corrections in the past" is no longer acceptable (Adler, 1975, p. 180).

Along the same lines, Berger (1989) refers to a number of studies conducted in the mid-1970s indicating the rise of female crime and delinquency and the emergence of a new type of female offender. This new 'woman' was more violent and aggressive than her predecessors. Within this new construction was the historical convergence of discursive practices labeling the female delinquent as abnormal and pathologically dangerous (highly sexualized). The explanations presented included; educational retardation, very poor homes, ungainly and masculine appearance, and deficient personalities. However, "the two factors pinpointed as having most significance—broken homes and psychiatric disorders—have consistently dominated theoretical attention, and have resulted in a projection of the delinquent girl as a deprived and inadequate individual" (Smith, 1978, p. 75).

In 1990, 50,000 women were arrested for aggravated assault (White and Kowalski, 1994). However, the impossibility or unacceptability of female 'aggression' suggests that it will go unnoticed and thus unnamed. "For this reason, female physical aggression seems more unexpected, becomes labeled irrational, and is denied legitimacy" (White and Kowalski, 1994, p. 488). It is important to note that the conclusions that men are more aggressive than women is interrupted and challenged as a gendered, reductionist, discursive practice. This practice results in the sexualization and institutionalization of female juvenile offenders as deviant rather than aggressive and delinquent. Even though, "the findings suggest that women have as much potential as men to be aggressive and that, given the appropriate circumstances, are as likely to display aggression as men . . ." (White and Kowalski, 1994, p. 490). Female aggression has become institutionalized within and against the regimes of truth of the patriarchal society. The myth of the nonaggressive woman that was constructed through sociohistorical discourses, such as the Progressive Era movements and the social institutions of the patriarchal family and legal system was reified through flawed research, according to White and Kowalski (1994). They state that because women committed fewer crimes than men they were seen as less aggressive, rather than seeing the ways women's aggressive behavior was circumscribed and limited to specific social situations. As a result, Fry and Gabriel (1994) highlight that Western scholarship and the construction of male aggression has framed aggression as a stable (masculine) category. Thus, the theories produced and the regimes of truth inscribed emerge from male-centered research. Aggression, therefore, is a gendered regime of truth and it insists on the binary of 'peacefulness.' For example, "some scholars argue that women are 'naturally' more inclined to peace and that motherhood provides an inherent ingredient for (female) pacifism" (Fry and Gabriel, 1994, p. 166).

The gendered nature of the regimes of truth that construct and perpetuate the public and private spaces of being for female juvenile offenders can be seen through recent studies of the myth of the 'body' and feminist research in general. This work shows how scientific and popular assumptions about natural sex differences have been used to justify social inequalities (Petersen and Davies, 1997). However, the regimes of truth that continue to shape the construction of the public and private spaces of being of female juvenile offenders as ungovernable, 'out-of-control,' highly sexualized girls requires interruption and serious interrogation. For example, research that studied male delinquency as explained by environmental factors continued to dominate while female delinquency was addressed in terms of stereotypical assumptions regarding their inherent biological or psychological nature (Berger, 1989). Explanations for female delinquency included a number of fascinating ideas, such as, an excess number of male chromosomes, lack of attractiveness and unsatisfying relationships with boys, and emotional dependency, loneliness, insecurity, and the trauma associated with the onset of menstruation. As mentioned earlier some researchers even suggested PMS as a cause (Berger, 1989). Central to this framing is the embodiment of the construction of female juvenile offenders within a discourse of crime—the body is fully present, the hysteria and irrationality of woman is accepted and the dependence on men/boys highlighted. Although attention has historically been focused on males, the recent change in the nature of offenses and the increasing number of females involved in armed robbery, gang violence, drug trafficking, etc., has led to some rather inconclusive theorizing on the subject. Recent research also includes focusing on dysfunctional families, victimization, aggression, neglect, rejection, physical and sexual abuse, self-perception, gender role and intellectual ability (Calhoun, Jurgens and Chen, 1993).

The Juvenile Justice System

Historically, the juvenile court law provided extensive powers of control and surveillance of female youth through the court and the work of police officials. Through the juvenile court system whole new areas of deviant behavior became subject to legal control. One of the most pervasive discourses framing female juvenile offenders continues to be the nature of offenses, for example, status offenses. It is important to define at this point the nature of the offenses that female juvenile offenders may be charged with. The 1987 Juvenile Detention and Correction Facility Census (JDCFC) defines 'delinquent offenses' as acts which would be considered crimes if committed by adults. 'Status offenses' are delinquent acts which would not be considered crimes if committed by adults such as truancy and running away (Calhoun, Jurgens and Chen, 1993; Chesney-Lind and Brown, 1999). Also being declared incorrigible youth was a major cause of youth, particularly girls, coming into contact with law enforcement (Chesney-Lind and Brown, 1999, p. 179). For example, in the early part of the twentieth century, premarital sex, flirting with sailors and staying out late were delinquent activities for which female minors faced arrest and detention and the juvenile court apprehended young females who violated prevailing moral codes (Odem and Schlossman, 1991). Contrary to popular belief, the law was not more benign when dealing with female youth. Females were more likely than males to be referred for status offenses; females often received harsher treatment for those status offenses than males received for serious offenses; and, this often included longer periods of institutionalization for females than for males (Sarri, 1983).

The historic development of the social institution of the Juvenile Justice System is also central to this discussion. Curran (1984) outlines three major historic periods in the 'handling' of female 'delinquents' ranging from a 'paternalistic' era prior, through a 'due process' era and finally emerging into a 'law and order' period in the late 1970s. "In other words, the tendency during this era was to maintain a clear 'double standard' in the courtroom with females often receiving harsher sentences for status-type offenses, like ungovernability, than males would receive for major delinquent offenses (Curran, 1984, p. 391). The liberalism of the 1960s was soon replaced with a more conservative 'get tough' attitude. A fascinating twist was the emergent 'liberation theory' that suggested the historical women's movement caused an increase in female crises as a result of gender role confusion. However, according to Curran (1984), the 'increase' was in the 1960s and was not a result of the increasing masculinization of young women but a reflection of a change in the legal reclassification of juvenile offenses.

However, in 2001, the American Bar Association and the National Bar Association published the *Justice by Gender* report. It called for an increased focus on the Juvenile Justice System with an emphasis on girls. According to the report, girls have received second-class treatment and historically have been neglected by the system (*Justice By Gender*, foreword). This report brings together many of the layered discourses I have highlighted earlier through the construction of institutional technologies of power. Thus by interspersing quotes from this very recent report I aimed to historicize this analysis. The report provides a useful example of the ways in which girls are framed as mysterious and different and thus the female juvenile offenders (bad girls) are beyond understanding. The deviant subject position is highlighted through philosophical, sexual, patriarchal and pathological discourses that are institutionalized in the Juvenile Justice System and other total social institutions, such as schools. Throughout the report legitimatized social constructions of adolescence and gender dominated. Thus, another layer of discourse was added to the mix; in this case a psychological or psychologizing discourse around adolescence. It is important to deconstruct the notions of gender and adolescence used in the report. In many ways the lack of critical analysis of populist notions of gender and adolescence is central to the im/possibility of 'homing' female juvenile offenders. The sociocultural institutions that 'house' and supposedly 'care' for these girls are constructed around reductive notions of gender, adolescence and other normalizing discourses. For example, a developmentally sound and culturally competent system of care emerges as a central idea. However, it is important to briefly wonder about the 'nature' of adolescence, as we have wandered through gender constructions earlier. In order to address the homelessness of female juvenile offenders we must discuss developmental and gender theories as social and historical construction (Adams, 1997). Indeed, further study on the stages of adolescence would be useful in this case if, as Davies and Adams (2000) suggest, "adolescents who exhibit the characteristics are normal, and adolescents who do not exhibit the characteristics are abnormal" (p. 18). Thus, another layer to the deviance of the subjectivity of female juvenile offenders is scaffolded.

Another theme that connects to Bhabha's (1994) work mentioned earlier is the call for suitable 'homes' framed as "an integrated system of care" in the report (*Justice by Gender*, 2001, p. 27). Such 'normal' and normalizing discourses of care are interrupted and resisted by the deviant subject position of the female juvenile offender. Therefore, the work presented here is important in its effort to interrupt the scaffolding of discourses that frame research concerning female juvenile offenders because such uninvestigated framing research assumptions are in danger of continuing to reduce the girls to deviant subject positions. Thus, the social institutions of the legal system and educational system regulating these constructions (engaged in the sociohistoric scaffolding of normalizing discourses) are unhomely spaces for these girls. The subject position itself is further reduced in the report to 'at-risk' and 'troubled' girls. This removal from 'normal' further suggests that the task or goal of the 'system' in dealing with and caring for such unusual 'girls' has been an ultimate failure. However, instead of calling for more studies of the institutions themselves, the report falls into a more comfortable position that reinforces the unarticulated assumptions of gender, citizenship and sexuality. The report highlights the lack of success in 'homing' the girls, drawing on examples of the failure of parental homes, the gendered nature of status offenses, the excessive detainment practices and contempt charges of the courts and the dismal state of detention facilities for girls without politicizing or historicizing the 'truth.'

It is critical that correctional practices and the practices of supporting social institutions such as our schools become responsive to adolescent females (Miller et al., 1999; Schaffner, Shick and Stein, 1997). Lawrence (1998) highlights the way the social institution responsible for educating children has been criticized for the repressive environment and the punitive actions by teachers. Whether the debate is on school funding, at-risk children, or pedagogy, the ways in which we think, talk and act around issues of 'good' girls and 'bad' girls through the construction of deviant behavior and the resultant legal classifications must be interrupted. Steet (1999) calls for a more sophisticated analysis of public education that addresses the technologies of power of schools as total institutions. She also highlights the need to consider the history of school reform and the history of public education and prisons in the United States. She states that these institutions are not isolated inventions "but an integral part of the story of compulsory education. And many of the struggles over reforms were essentially the same struggles carried out in the public schools and prisons between conflicting political, philosophical, and pedagogical ideas" (Steet, 1999, p. 44).

There is also a need to complicate the study of female juvenile offenders by situating it in contemporary social reforms and critical movements. Ageton (1983) presents a historical discussion of the dynamics of female delinquency from 1976–1980 that highlights the lack of theorizing about female juvenile delinquency in the light of new social reforms and factors such as the women's movement, increasing numbers of women in the workforce and the Equal Rights Amendment debate. She is responding to the populist belief that the situation is getting worse—the crisis talk and the dominating regimes of truth—that the 'bad' minority and lower-class deviant girls are an increasing threat to society. Writings on this topic tend to be highly moralistic in tone and based on commonsense and sexist assumptions (Smith, 1978, p. 74).

> Today, correctional programs for women lag far behind those of their male counterparts. In the past, women traditionally provided a 'civilizing influence' on society; thus when they broke the law, they were viewed as going against their very nature. Girls and women who committed crimes were figuratively 'fallen angels,' considered to be so depraved, that there was no hope of redemption; therefore, educational programs for them were deemed unnecessary (Freedman, 1981) (Miller et al., 1997, p. 231).

Schools, parent homes, foster homes and the Juvenile Justice System—all these 'homes' exclude the deviant girls from belonging as they trouble, interrupt and even reject the normalized construction of 'female,' 'good girl' and 'good child.' By analyzing the intersections of historical discourses constructing the female juvenile offender as deviant, this paper highlighted the im/possibility of 'home,' that is, the 'unhomely spaces' of the social institutions catering to these girls and the homelessness of the deviant girl within and against the hegemonic discourses. Some of the historical discourse 'themes/truths' discussed included: philosophizing discourses of 'good girl' and 'good child' that play out in the construction of socially acceptable (normalized) gender roles; the construction of female aggression as deviant; the sexualizing of female juvenile offenders and pathologizing of deviant behavior; the institutional discourses and technologies of power that used harsher restrictions and detainment practices to regulate the female juvenile offenders. If we then consider the constructions of gender and adolescence embedded in the most recent report (*Justice by Gender*, 2001) addressing the failure of the 'system,' we are faced with the impossibility of socially acceptable female deviant or aggressive behavior. We are also faced with the effects of power of the epistemic violence arising from the reductive nature of gendered social roles. The tension is that the notions of 'caring' and 'homing' inherent in the social institutions of the schools, the Juvenile Justice System and institutions of detention are often reduced to a more punitive disciplining approach to female juvenile offenders. The total social institutions continue to work from normalized and exclusivist constructions of adolescence and 'good girls/good citizen.'

> School officials are often the first contact these young women have with the legal system. In some instances, schools work in conjunction with the juvenile courts, beginning with truancy proceedings, to ensure an early identification of potential juvenile offenders and a smooth transition of violent and aggressive teens from school disciplinary proceedings to juvenile court proceedings (Michaelis, 1999, p. 8).

School officials include teachers, administrators, school secretaries, bus drivers and custodians, to name a few. They are the first 'state agent' to be called upon to determine, interpret and apply how the rules and laws of the court system fit the situation at hand. Thus they 'announce' the state law—and determine the public and private spaces of being for female juvenile offenders (Michaelis, 1999). School officials and judges create the narrative—the 'truth' of the rules and laws for the deviant girls (Michaelis, 1999, p. 15). Thus, by historicizing the deviant subjectivity of female juvenile offenders we may provide a space for research that is less unhomely, research that attends to the possibility of interrupting the way institutions of detention and education, emancipatory research and prevention reforms have reduced and excluded these girls. Indeed, using the in-between or third space suggested by Bhabha (1994) and the work of Ong (1995), 'home' may be redefined more hopefully as an intersection of motion and dwelling that is fluid and partial, thus reminding us of the need to remain suspicious of essentializing assumptions embedded in cultural representation, space and place.

Theorizing the Raced Construction of the Subject in Multicultural Education

Just as the normalizing discourses surrounding juvie girls may be analyzed using Curriculum Spaces Research Theory, the raced nature of multicultural education may also be informed/interrogated from this viewpoint. I have included this discussion in this chapter in order to highlight the usefulness of analyzing discourses that are often assumed to be transformative and yet are in danger of reinscribing normalizing practices. Multicultural education discourses are in danger of including uninterrogated raced constructions of "citizen" as illustrated in the talk of "whiteness" that is currently circulating. Therefore, another way of analyzing the assimilationist tendencies of multicultural education is to study the Curriculum Spaces that legitimize the dominant perspective and limit the effectiveness of this transformative effort.

Multicultural education is often accused of becoming an assimilated modernist project. Interestingly enough, it is also decried by conservatives and radicals alike. Yet there remains a place within this field to interrupt positions of privilege and provide spaces from which to work against normalizing institutional and pedagogical practices that reinforce the epistemological position of whiteness without question. One of the problems, according to West (1993), is that "Conservative behaviorists talk about attitudes and values as if political and economic structures hardly exist." Ladson-Billings (1995) also reflects upon this when she talks of the ways in which courses in multicultural education engender resistance and reinforce stereotypes. Such courses, according to Ladson-Billings, are seen as lacking in intellectual rigor and merely supported to mollify those racialized "Others." Discussing the foundations of the multicultural education movement as arising from the Civil Rights Movement, she highlights how race "has moved off the page" as the central construct.

Recent discussion in multicultural education has highlighted the ways in which the social construction of whiteness has been concealed in our educational discourse (McLaren, 1997; Frankenburg, 1993; Sleeter, 1994). Using the lens of a poststructural analysis, this racial construction may be seen as an aspect of the dominant social discourse within the modernist knowledge project (Lincoln, 1998). The modernist knowledge project works (a) to produce socially legitimate knowledge that may essentialize difference and exclude marginalized groups from positions of empowerment through stereotypical representations of culturally different Others, and (b) from within realist ontological assumptions. A poststructural perspective, however, may suggest alternative counterhegemonic subject constructions that could work within and against exclusive notions of "citizen" in this area.

Popkewitz (1998c), discussed earlier, suggests that the redemptive culture of the social and human sciences has not only created docile bodies but also inscribed theoretical and pedagogical reforms as for the "good" of society through the development of a "good" citizen. In this way, the modernist project has constructed socially, historically, politically and economically what a "good" citizen is and thus excluded marginalized Others from positions of privilege by their race, class, gender and/or other standpoints of "difference."

Cultural Performance and Hegemonic Structures. As I discussed in chapter two, bringing the literature from anthropology and cultural studies to bear on this discussion is one way to study how culture (and cultural subjects/citizens) are sociohistorically constructed. From this perspective, culture is performed through social interactions often involving experiences of domination and subordination within the Enlightenment project of colonization and imperialist territorialization. Clifford (1997), Bhabha (1994), Pratt (1992), Kaplan (1996) and Gilroy (1993) have discussed how culture is a performative act that is socially and politically inscribed. According to Clifford (1997), how one knows and engages in social interactions (as evidenced through ethnographic study) is also culturally performative. Culture is, accordingly, an embodied act influenced by a variety of forces, including sociohistorical, political and economic influences. Paul Gilroy (1993) discusses the diasporic nature of the construction of the black Atlantic and disrupts the notions of cultural holism or racial essentialism through a discussion of the ways in which cultural performance is influenced by sociohistorical conditions and political and economic influences—using music to discuss the multiple origins of the music of the "West."

A number of other theorists also discuss the socially interactive performative nature of culture as a place from which to disrupt the colonizing mentality and the legitimization of the Western regimes of truth (Pratt, 1992; Kaplan, 1996; Gilroy, 1993; Bhabha, 1994). In *The Location of Culture,* Bhabha (1994) highlights the reinscription of hegemonic discourse through the relativistic discourse of diversity. He suggests that by highlighting the hybridity of cultural performance we may move beyond the essentialist discussions of race and culture. For culture, according to Bhabha, is developed performatively through discursive processes. Bhabha aims to disrupt the epistemological assumptions of the hegemonic discourse that silences and erases issues of race from any discussion of culture. He stresses especially the need to focus upon *difference* rather than on *diversity* in that this term has become a culturally relativistic position—a White solution to the 'Black problem.' Sleeter (1994), McLaren (1997), and Frankenberg (1993) all call for the study of underlying epistemological assumptions and normalizing practices of anti-racist and multicultural education in order to work against the assimilationist tendencies of institutionalized efforts. From this perspective, Whiteness is a culturally constructed epistemological position of dominance effectively Othering all considered non-white. It creates the effect of power that excludes through objectifying and pathologizing their racial constructions. The epistemology of whiteness is a culturally advantaged standpoint from which to maintain positions of privilege and power.

Lorde (1984), Franklin (1993), and hooks (1989) talk back to interrupt such dominant perspectives. Lorde (1984) sums it up when she states that "the oppressors maintain their position and evade responsibility for their own actions" (p. 115). By making invisible the ways in which the dominant position has been reinscribed through even well-intentioned pedagogical reforms, whiteness has been uninterrogated as a position of privileged cultural performance. Franklin (1993) believes that the reason we have failed to create a color-blind society is because it is not in "our" (white people's) best interests to do so. He calls for an investigation of our past, our race, our dominant whiteness. "The final reason a color-blind society eludes us is that we do not wish to find it. A balkanized racial differentiation has been remarkably profitable and even satisfying to many people" (Franklin, 1993, p. 50). hooks (1989) also talks back, using "the margins" as a position of power reflecting counterhegemonic discourse, and calls for a collective effort involving radical black women, people of color and white people to work to end white supremacy.

Frankenberg (1993) and Sleeter (1994) suggest that studying and troubling whiteness will allow whites involved in anti-racist and multicultural education to reconceptualize their place in the process. Sleeter suggests that, "White people have a good deal of knowledge about racism: all of us have been well socialized to be racists, and benefit from racism constantly. I would like Whites to articulate, examine, question, and critique what we know about racism" (Sleeter, 1994, p. 5). Defining whiteness is central in any discussion that attempts to trouble this normative, reductionist subject construction. McLaren (1997) defines it as follows:

> Whiteness is a sociohistorical form of consciousness, given at birth at the nexus of capitalism, colonial rule, and the emergent relationships among dominant and subordinate groups....Whiteness is also a refusal to acknowledge how white people are implicated in certain social relations of privilege and relations of domination and subordination (p. 9).

By utilizing the conception of cultural performance, we can move beyond dominant erasures of difference to interrogate the ways in which we know ourselves in discourses framing multicultural education and in social education in general. According to Sleeter (1994), "By white racism (or white supremacy) I am referring to the system of rules, procedures, and tacit beliefs that result in Whites collectively maintaining control over the wealth and power of the nation and the world" (p. 6).

Whiteness and Assimilation as Discursive Practices. Ladson-Billings (1995) describes the myth of the "Unity of Difference" discourse in the field and talks of the ways in which multicultural education has been co-opted and the way "race has moved off the page" even though multicultural education developed from the efforts of the Civil Rights Movement to address race in educational settings. Race remains untheorized and undertheorized. "Celebratory Multicultural Education provides schools with convenient escapes from the worrisome concerns of race and racism" (Ladson-Billings, 1995, pp. 10–11). There is a call for professional organizations to act now to move within and against the dominant subject constructions in multicultural education to reclaim the possibility of a more adequate knowing/being in transformative discursive practices by articulating the oppressive race/ing of citizenship (Ladson-Billings, 1995; Sleeter, 1994). By defining something previously unarticulated, whiteness may be interrogated as a standpoint of privilege, a structural advantage, and a place from which to Other all those considered non-

Gender and Race

white. "Whiteness changes over time and space and is in no way a transhistorical essence. Rather, as I have argued, it is a complexly constructed product of local, regional, national, and global relations, past and present" (Frankenberg, 1993, p. 236). This point of entry into a historically Othered and marginalized discursive practice suggests there are distinct possibilities for interrupting the dominant curative and assimilationist multicultural education project:

> There is, however, one racial subject where an upsurge of interest by academics may precede and effectively recast public formulations of race problems: that is the matter of whiteness. Through the efforts of literary and film critics, historians, sociologists, and gradually, anthropologists, whiteness, as an analytical object, is being established as a powerful means of critiquing the reproduction and maintenance of systems of racial inequality, within the United States and around the Globe (Hartigan, 1999, p. 184).

Further interrupting the conceptualization of race as a natural construct (somehow distorted by racism), Britzman (1998) suggests that the ahistorical educational desire to simplify complex histories of racism denies or refuses the effects of power through the normalization of gender and race.

> The normalization of race—like the normalization of gender and sex—as an obvious, visible, and predictive feature of the body is thus a discourse that gestures to the problem of the production by mechanisms of power that incite proper and improper bodies (p. 105).

By studying the normalizing, uninterrupted discourse practices of social education as illustrative of the refusals/silent exclusions of citizenship, Britzman opens a space for a discussion of the exclusionary practices that support/create/construct the concept of citizen.

Delgado (1999) also historicizes exclusionary practices in the social construction of citizenship in his discussion of the raced nature of the citizen as part of a national community:

> In the United States, the current community—the institution to which the argument would hand unfettered discretion regarding immigration policy— is deeply affected by racism and exclusionary practices. For much of our history, a national-origin quota system and, before that, anti-Asian and anti-Mexican laws, kept the immigrants of color low... For much of our history, women and blacks were denied the right to vote or hold office. Higher

education was virtually closed to both until about 1960, and in Southern states, Black Codes made it a crime to teach a black to read....'The community,' then, is deeply shaped by racism, sexism, and xenophobia. This is not only in terms of its demography and makeup but also its preferences and values (p. 250).

In a similar vein, Rosaldo (1999) highlights the universalization of the concept of citizen as founded upon abstract notions of theoretical universality in tension with the substantive level of exclusionary, marginalizing practices. Rosaldo goes on to state that "even in its late-eighteenth-century Enlightenment origins, citizenship in the republic differentiated men of privilege from the rest, second-class citizens and non-citizens" (p. 253). While it seems as if this historically abstract conceptualization of citizen is easily deconstructed I suggest here that the ways in which power/knowledge construct the "good" citizen in social education discourses are less visible and more dangerously exclusivist. The refusals of citizenship suggest that there is a "normal" or "proper" embodiment of the concept that manifests in discursive practices. This normalization produces and excludes, in the cases presented here, in a number of different ways. First, through gendering and scientizing teacher education reform, and second, by racing multicultural education discourse as an assimilationist project.

Ong (1999) outlines citizenship in a similar fashion. Ong presents it as a subject-ification, in the Foucauldian sense, through "self-making and being-made by power relations that produce consent through schemes of surveillance, discipline, control and administration...(Ong, 1999, p. 263). She goes on to define governmentality as aimed at giving a unifying expression to the multi-faceted and differential experiences of groups within society. "This role of the state in universalizing citizenship is paradoxically attained through a process of individuation whereby people are constructed in definitive and specific ways as citizens—taxpayers, workers, consumers, and welfare dependents" (pp. 263—264). Therefore, the work of Ong (1999) and Popkewitz (1998a) connects social education discourses with the tensions between the social administration of freedom and state "agencies." They suggest that the pragmatic struggle towards understanding citizenship also calls for critical analysis of the regulatory regimes in state agencies and civil society. Ong (1999) states:

Gender and Race

Indeed, it is precisely in liberal democracies like the United States that the governmentality of state agencies is often discontinuous, even fragmentary, and the work of instilling proper normative behavior and identity in newcomers must also be taken up by institutions in civil society. For instance, hegemonic ideas about belonging and not belonging in racial and cultural terms often converge in state and non-state institutional practices through which subjects are shaped in ways that are at once specific and diffuse. These are the ideological fields within which different criteria of belonging on the basis of civilized conduct by categorically distinguishable (dominant) others become entangled with culture, race and class….(p. 264).

The work of Britzman (1998), Popkewitz (1998b, 2000), and Ong (1999) suggests connections between social constructions of race and gender and the normalizing discourses discussed by Foucault (1977). Britzman (1998) highlights how the "normal" version of anti-racist pedagogy (i.e., multicultural education) relies on humanistic constructs or role models and self-esteem building and seems to forget the problem of group identification and disassociation from the question/possibility of difference. For example, the tensions exist within discussions of difference, she suggests, between African Americans and Jews as mainstream debates in this area are often collapsed into the imperatives of whiteness or get stuck in the binary of assimilation or authenticity.

Britzman (1998) suggests that if we accept that efforts at anti-racist pedagogy are inconsolable, that they are embedded within complex social constructions of race, difference and normalcy, then we should engage with what it excludes or refuses: "This is not a move towards a new inclusivity, even though opening the stakes of identification and learning from the conflicts within communities should trouble what is imagined as a normal race or, more pertinently, as a normal representation of race" (p. 111).

Spaces of Othering through Gender and Race

The maps drawn about children are not neutral but are practices that divide and normalize. That is, the distinctions that order children's capabilities function to divide membership and nonmembership along a continuum of value through which individual capability and competence are constructed. The categories of learning, for example, are inserted as part of ways to 'reason' about educational phenomena and to differentiate between children through an unspoken normalization about the capabilities of those who can 'learn,' and those 'at risk' of failure (Popkewitz, 2000, p. 22).

This chapter has outlined a few of the ways the effects of power normalize the subject construction of "good girl" and "good citizen" for juvie girls and the ways multicultural education is raced as a major concern for the field of social education. In multicultural education the assimilationist tendencies of the institutionalization of the field seem to reflect a normative racialized construction of the "good" citizen that is framed within a dominant uninterrogated discourse of whiteness. The resultant discursive practices suggest that this area is focused on "difference" that actually produces regimes of truth legitimizing the dominant and (thus) Othering those students who are visibly "different" or "raced."

By re-conceptualizing and interrupting the assumed "neutrality" of the field I suggest we may complicate our understanding of how discourses and governing practices (Foucault's governmentalities) are produced as Curriculum Spaces within a populist rhetoric of redemption that is not necessarily liberatory:

> Curriculum as a governing practice becomes almost self-evident as we think of the 'making' of the proper citizen. This citizen is one who has the correct dispositions, sensitivities and awareness to act as a self-governing individual in the new political, cultural and economic contexts. Current reforms that focus on 'constructivist pedagogy' and teacher education reforms that considered the 'beliefs' and dispositions' of the teacher are the secularization of the confessional systems of self discipline and control (Popkewitz, 1998a, p. 89).

The normalizing practices of discursively produced Curriculum Spaces embedded within pedagogy and curriculum development should be studied in social education to address the tensions that exist between social administration and freedom in liberal democracies (Popkewitz, 1998c). The exemplars offered here highlight the institutionalized nature of the discursive production of curriculum spaces. It is the responsibility of all of us to understand how these constructions shape the decisions we make as stakeholders and gatekeepers of curriculum.

5
A Postcolonial Subject Position

And now to the personal/professional, local level of knowing. This chapter presents a personal journey that is framed by a particular historical moment—9/11. It is an exemplar at the level of the personal or local subject position and draws heavily upon postcolonial elements of the colonizing epistemologies inherent in Curriculum Spaces Research Theory. Thus, the aim is to highlight the fluidity of Curriculum Spaces and suggests a sense of negotiation. This is an important move because it calls for a complication of our understanding of power and then suggests we work to interrupt the effects of power as they play out in our lives. Thus, spaces of negotiation are described as im/possible constructions with intersecting discourses (Bhabha, 1994; Pratt, 1992; Spivak, 1993). The way we know is often obscured by the effects of power and this chapter is an attempt to reveal how the intersecting discourses played out on one body—my body. And, in conclusion, we must go back to the beginning, the arrivals of theoretical development that frame this personal journey.

This exemplar brings together a number of perspectives and ways of looking at 'Curriculum Spaces' in order to complicate the effects of the current crisis of national security that has developed in response to the events of 9/11. First, the crisis reproduction of an exclusive binary of 'good'/Pro-American citizen and 'bad'/Anti-American Alien is presented as the impetus for this need to redefine curriculum spaces in the post-9/11 era. Second, I highlight the Curriculum Spaces made possible and impossible within the intersecting discourses that have emerged. Third, I present an autobiographical response with implications for living in 'Curriculum Spaces' in this historic moment.

9/11 Otherness

In the various texts that emerged from/after/throughout the historic moment of what has come to be called '9/11,' there has been an unapologetic Othering occurring.

> The United States government, like others, primarily responds to centers of concentrated domestic power. That should be a truism. Of course, there are other influences, including popular currents—that is true of all societies,

even brutal totalitarian systems, and surely more democratic ones. Insofar as we have information, the U.S. government is now trying to exploit the opportunity to ram through its own agenda: militarization, including 'missile defense,' code words for militarization of space; undermining social democratic programs; also undermining concerns over the harsh effects of corporate 'globalization,' or environmental issues, or health insurance, and so on; instituting measures that will intensify the transfer of wealth to the very few (for example, eliminating corporate taxes); and regimenting society, so as to eliminate public debate and protest (Chomsky, 2001, p. 33–34).

Chomsky (2001) suggests there are different ways the national security agenda has manifested itself in pubic and private spaces. *The New Yorker Magazine* (September 16, 2002) presented an issue devoted to the historic moment. One of the articles in the issue presented a summary of commentary texts that emerged after 9/11 with a brief discussion (or dismissal) of each (Menand, 2002). Included in this collection was the work of Noam Chomsky presented above. His work is presented in the group labeled 'anti-American' and he is joined by Gore Vidal and Alice Walker (albeit Walker's work is considered more consolatory). According to Menand (2002), the social commentary texts of Jean Baudrillard and Slavoj Zizek are also anti-American but provide a more 'European' perspective that suggests bin Laden is a modernist creation and the result of global capitalism and suggests that this is not necessarily the time for another paradigm but rather a time for action—action against global capitalism (p. 101). There are a number of other texts mentioned in this article highlighting other perspectives, but in the final accounting they are presented as either anti-American or pro-American celebrations of the moment. The writing of Hugh Downs, Dinesh D'Souza, William Bennett, and Roger Rosenblatt are presented as Pro-American (Menand, 2002). There are so many contradictory discourses emerging that Menand (2002) concludes with a paradox:

> If you try to link these responses in a formula, you get something like: Americans are willing to fight, and even die, for the belief that no one should be made to die for belief. And: Americans hold it to be a transcendant truth that it is possible to live a good life without loyalty to a transcendent cause. The formulations are fuzzy because 'a way of life' has many aspects. There is no perfect clarity. Let us be clear about that (p. 104).

The representations and commentaries discussed above suggest that we are currently in a state-of-flux that reinscribes some ways of being while also providing possibilities for interruption. The spaces made possible in this historical postmodern moment require a different way of thinking. "Conflict, condemnation, fear, and militarism dominate the airwaves; prophetic voices are silenced and meaningful notions of hope are muted. We live in dangerous times, and we also live at a moment of incredible opportunity" (Slattery and Rapp, 2002, p. 229).

Colonized and Colonizing Spaces

We are faced with a moment where 'the person-is-political' and 'the-world-is-in-the-home' (Bhabha, 1994). Bhabha (1994) demands we take measure of how we dwell at 'home' while producing an image of world history. Therefore, as we watched the events of 9/11 unfold through the media and invited (or were confronted with) the world in our homes, we were also producing an image of world history as an effect of power. When we move this notion of 'home' into the Curriculum Spaces we inhabit within and against the U.S. academy and more specifically, the undergraduate and graduate classrooms, we seem to face an interruption of 'home' when we attempt to highlight or discuss the paradoxical nature of the historic moment. Further, it seems as if any attempt at interruption or counterhegemonic discourse is immediately framed as suspect and 'anti-American' in these spaces.

I believe it is useful to consider these Curriculum Spaces as 'in-between' (Bhabha, 1994):

> What is theoretically innovative, and politically crucial, is the need to think beyond narratives of originary and initial subjectivities and to focus on those moments or processes that are produced in the articulation of cultural differences. These 'in-between' spaces provide the terrain for elaborating strategies of selfhood—singular or communal—that initiate new signs of identity, and innovative sites of collaboration, and contestation, in the act of defining the idea of society itself (Bhabha, 1994, p. 2).

Bhabha (1994) goes on to describe the in-between space as emerging in the interstices, with the overlap and displacement of difference, where the collective experiences of nationness, community interest and cultural value are negotiated. The question that is central here is "How are subjects formed 'in-between', or in excess of, the sum of the 'parts' of difference (usually intoned as race/class/gender, etc.)?" (p. 2).

The idea of the unhomely space is also important as it adds to the possibilities for redefining Curriculum Spaces in the dangerous historic moment:

> The negating activity is, indeed, the intervention of the 'beyond' that establishes a boundary: a bridge, where 'presencing' begins because it captures something of the estranging sense of the relocation of the home and the world—the unhomeliness—that is the condition of extra-territorial and cross-cultural initiations. To be unhomed is not to be homeless, nor can the 'unhomely' be easily accommodated in that familiar division of social life into private and public spheres (Bhabha, 1994 , p. 9).

So, how might we redefine these spaces and notions with the aim of providing a more complicated knowing with possibilities for interruption and learning. Pratt (1992) provides one way of 'seeing' these spaces in her conceptualization of 'contact zones.'

> One coinage that recurs throughout the book is the term 'contact zone,' which I use to refer to the space of colonial encounters, the space in which peoples geographically and historically separated come into contact with each other and establish ongoing relations, usually involving conditions of coercion, radical inequality, and intractable conflict (Pratt, 1992, p. 6).

According to Pratt (1992), 'contact zones' occur when colonialist selves meet/conquer/silence/erase Other less powerful selves. This is a "production of spaces in which economic exploitation and erasure of all those Othered may then occur (Pratt, 1992, p. 201). What does this suggest for Curriculum Spaces? It suggests that classroom discussion, interruption and questioning exist within a social project framed by conditions of coercion, radical inequality and intractable conflict. According to Pratt, the effects of power are visited upon the bodies of those inhabiting the Curriculum Space in the spatial and temporal corpescence of the subject. Pratt's (1992) work is useful here because it highlights and foregrounds how this plays out in Curriculum Spaces as an interactive and improvisational dimension so easily ignored or suppressed by diffusionist accounts of conquest and domination (p. 7).

This is another useful idea for it highlights the interconnectedness of the spaces while centering issues of power and coercion. This is a vital point of my entry into the current post-9/11 historical moment.

A Postcolonial Subject Position

By considering the effects of power and how they play out we can reveal previously obscured discourses and manifestations of power. From the erasure of Others to the construction of the good citizen as opposed to the binary opposite of 'dangerous Alien.'

In the section that follows I attempt to historicize the concept of 'citizen' in an effort to reveal the exclusivities that result in the normalized construction of the 'good' and orderly citizen. This is framed in this historical moment—as one who does not interrupt or question. By studying this we might then move beyond oppositional counter-narratives toward a more critical intimacy and a more adequate knowing (Britzman, 1998).

Citizens and Aliens

In chapter three I presented an exemplar that discussed the normalizing, uninterrupted discourse practices of social education as illustrative of the refusals/silent exclusions of citizenship (Cary, 2001). What is interesting to note here is that in that discussion a number of historical frames that made possible the subject position of 'good citizen' today in the United State were presented. Revisiting that work here, in light of the events of 9/11, I believe it is central to how we might know and interrupt the current dualisms that exist. Drawing upon the work of Britzman (1998), Delgado (1999), Ong (1999), Rosaldo (1999) and Popkewitz (1998c), provided a particular curriculum space for a discussion of the exclusionary practices that support/create/construct the concept of citizen.

For example, Delgado (1999) historicized exclusionary practices that produce the social construction of citizenship as follows:

> In the United States, the current community—the institution to which the argument would hand unfettered discretion regarding immigration policy—is deeply affected by racism and exclusionary practices. For much of our history, a national-origin quota system and, before that, anti-Asian and anti-Mexican laws, kept the immigrants of color low... For much of our history, women and blacks were denied the right to vote or hold office. Higher education was virtually closed to both until about 1960, and in Southern states, Black Codes made it a crime to teach a black to read...'The community,' then, is deeply shaped by racism, sexism, and xenophobia. This is not only in terms of its demography and makeup but also its preferences and values (p. 250).

This work makes central the issue of race and Rosaldo (1999) also highlighted the way this subject position is framed by exclusionary and marginalizing practices. "Even in its late-eighteenth-century Enlightenment origins, citizenship in the republic differentiated men of privilege from the rest, second-class citizens and non-citizens" (p. 253). The subject position of the 'good citizen suggests there is a "normal" or "proper" embodiment of the concept that manifests in discursive practices. This normalization produces and excludes.

Ong (1999) describes the construction of citizenship as subjectification. Drawing upon the Foucauldian notion of "self-making and being-made by power relations that produce consent through schemes of surveillance, discipline, control and administration...(Ong, 1999, p. 263). Indeed, both Ong (1999) and Popkewitz (1998c) connect social education discourses with the tensions between the social administration of freedom and state "agencies." They suggest that the pragmatic struggle toward understanding citizenship calls for critical analysis of the regulatory regimes in state agencies and civil society. It's all about belonging and not-belonging, and citizens and Aliens. Ong (1999) states:

> Indeed, it is precisely in liberal democracies like the United States that the governmentality of state agencies is often discontinuous, even fragmentary, and the work of instilling proper normative behavior and identity in newcomers must also be taken up by institutions in civil society. For instance, hegemonic ideas about belonging and not belonging in racial and cultural terms often converge in state and non-state institutional practices through which subjects are shaped in ways that are at once specific and diffuse. These are the ideological fields within which different criteria of belonging on the basis of civilized conduct by categorically distinguishable (dominant) others become entangled with culture, race and class... (p. 264)

To bring this to bear on the discussion of Curriculum Spaces, Popkewitz (1998c) discusses the ways the subject position of 'good' citizen becomes constructed as self-evident and the only 'proper' manifestation of the position. When you connect this with Chomsky's concern regarding the regimented society we now inhabit, this issue is worth considering. Popkewitz (1998c) also addresses this when he states:

> Curriculum as a governing practice becomes almost self-evident as we think of the 'making' of the proper citizen. This citizen is one who has the correct dispositions, sensitivities and awareness to act as a self-governing individual in the new political, cultural and economic contexts. Current

A Postcolonial Subject Position

reforms that focus on 'constructivist pedagogy' and teacher education reforms that considered the 'beliefs and dispositions' of the teacher are the secularization of the confessional systems of self discipline and control (Popkewitz, 1998a, p. 89).

In later work Popkewitz (2000) describes the project of the social sciences in this country as actually organizing "the thinking, feeling, hoping, and 'knowing' capacities of the productive citizen" (p. 19). According to Popkewitz (200) schooling and what I am calling here—Curriculum Spaces—historically aimed to develop a collective social identity and citizenship that embodied notions of the "Americanization" of immigrants and a universalized image of the child through curriculum social efficiency movements (Popkewitz, 2000). What is the aim now? I believe it is vital to investigate social practice and subject relations as represented and representing in discourse practices. The following autobiographical presentation is an attempt to do just that through the lens of the in-between Curriculum Spaces.

A Postcolonial Story

This section of this piece emerged from various moments of angst and alienation that occurred within my personal/professional Curriculum Spaces following the horror of '9/11.' When I first arrived in the United States in 1999 I had been quite content with my 'comfortable distance' from the ideological aggressivity of the U.S. academy (McCannell, 1994). I attempted to use my Curriculum Space as one of interrogation of the imperialist project of this benevolent Superpower and I playfully situated myself as an Alien outside of the political and nationalistic regimes of truth that framed the academy.

And then 9/11 happened and I was no longer able nor did anyone have the right to be so 'comfortable.' I had always found my accent and ability as a native English speaker produced certain advantages even within my oppositional Alien subject position. Suddenly, after 9/11, the curriculum spaces where I had played within and against the dominant culture by using my privileged White, English speaker self was in danger. In fact it was re-framed as a dangerous position. My previously non-threatening, amusing Australian 'colonial cousin' subject self (Cary, 1999a) was framed with all of my sister and brother Aliens, as 'dangerous outsider.' We were within the dualism of citizenship as outsider, dangerous, Alien. Paradoxically, at the same time, I came to realize I was much more invested in this U.S. nation-space than I had realized. So, my desire to belong was now at odds with the impossibility of belonging. What's that all about?

The following excerpt was written in the months following 9/11. The event itself occurred the day after the events of 9/11. It suggests an autobiographical Curriculum Space that addresses the ways in which the current national security 'crisis' talk, and the dualisms of belonging and not-belonging in the moment frame the possibilities of being and reduce the spaces of resistance and refusal (Britzman, 1998; Giroux, 2002).

> *Wednesday, September 12, 2001*
> *I stood in front of the class today and did not know what to say… A graduate level education class at a research university and I was silent. How was I to teach in this space? As a scholar of postcolonial and postmodern theories of education—how was I to connect my work to the horrific reality we faced? The 'real' was so violent and coercive. And, as a 'guest' of the INS—how much space did I have? How would this event redefine the power relationship in my classroom— would a student use the 'anti-American' defense against unwanted critiques of the educational project—would they go to the administration with their accusations? How much 'hope' was there for critical intimacy or post-critical dialogue now? This is a global moment yet I am a postcolonial scholar living in an inscribed national space.*

Reflected in this excerpt are issues of not-belonging, Alienness, outsiderness, danger, violence, total institutions of education and immigration. The Curriculum Spaces presented here are contact zones and in-between spaces. They are unhomely moments. And it is not over. Time has passed but the Curriculum Spaces we inhabit are still being framed by this historical event. These were some of the questions I faced on that first day after the tragedy of 9/11 and they still affect my life, my teaching, and my being/knowing in Curriculum Spaces. The immediacy and urgency have faded but the 'lesson' of the time is poignant. Since then I have often found myself so aware of the inherent 'dangers' of my critical and poststructural (untenured) stance in the university classroom—that I have silenced my 'self.' However, as an academic committed to asking difficult questions and entering dangerous pedagogical terrain, this self-regulation and surveillance produced a particular effect of power. I was in danger of getting lost within (and NOT against) the total institution of the U.S. academy. The question is—how can we use such spaces for critical intimacy so that getting lost is not a bad thing (Lather, 2001a)?

A Postcolonial Subject Position

Over the last decade or so I have been an expatriot. I have worked, studied, researched, and taught outside of Australia. Thus, I have benefited from the exotic space of the Australian academic in both Canada and the United States of America. Australians, as a stereotyped group, seemed to be welcomed and exoticized. For example, my accent was considered 'cute' (almost 'British'—a colonially desirable accent). Often I was told that my accent made me sound more authoritative—anglophilia is rampant in the academy. I actually benefited from the exclusivist dominant constructions of race and language in this country (Sleeter, 1994; McLaren, 1997; Frankenberg, 1993). As a White, Australian Alien I was not as threatening as my sister and brother Aliens who were visibly different and had 'less-desirable' accents.

Then came '9/11.' Although I had always known I was playing here as a 'guest' of the INS, I was immediately reminded of my 'guest' status. And for a time after September 11 it seemed to me that the space for Other ways of being and Other perspectives was greatly reduced and my own vulnerability as 'outsider' increased (Giroux, 2002). However, this is where the many layers of the social discourses erupt and disrupt. Even faced with my continuing/current Alien vulnerability, I am still a White professor, and therefore I am sometimes considered less 'suspect' than those of my fellow international colleagues who were visibly different. As a native English speaker I am objectified as a more 'acceptable' Alien (if there is such a thing) compared to those who are clearly Othered—shaped by the assumption that English is a superior language (Macedo, 1998).

> Maintained is the status quo that functions as a cultural reproduction mechanism which systematically does not allow other cultural subjects, who are considered outside the mainstream, to be present in history. These cultural subjects who are profiled as the 'other' are but palely represented in history within our purportedly democratic society (Macedo, 1998, p. 261).

Finally, as a highly educated individual I believe I am continuing to successfully negotiate the total social institution—and yet I still feel vulnerable.

Why am I so fearful? Because previously 'safe' critical spaces seem to have disappeared. As a non-citizen I do not have 'inalienable' rights. As an Alien—I am suspect. How we define citizenship in times of crisis is limiting and exclusivist (Popkewitz, 1998c; Cary, 2001). As Giroux (2002) states "There is little leeway for a vocabulary of political or social transformation" (p. 27). Indeed, there is little leeway for those of us (and there are a large number of 'foreign' scholars teaching, researching and writing in this country) who are non-citizens to engage in such historical moments without risk—either in our classrooms, in our writings, or on campus. The private/public space and the personal/professional space have been redefined and re-historicized. Giroux's (2002) call for continued efforts to interrupt the neo-liberal and militaristic discourse is risky business for all, but even more risky for Others.

Alien professors work within a space that is not indeterminate or unsubscribed (Spivak, 1993). What risks do I take in speaking out? With the new laws will I become suspect (Giroux, 2002)? How safe is *this* space for wondering about difference in a time of national crisis? How does crisis talk simplify and reduce the issues to 'manageable' bits/bytes?

My personal negotiation of the Curriculum Spaces discussed above are defined by a patriarchal, gendered civil society and the subject position of 'alien' is always/already at risk of supplementarity (Bhabha, 1994). Therefore, as I continue to negotiate and work through this horrific historic moment and the ideological aggressivity of the total institution, I will always already redraw my space of resistance by highlighting the normalizing effects of crisis talk and by teaching with courage (Labaree, 1995: Foucault, 1977). The autobiographical presentation above is an attempt to use the in-between, openly highlight the 'unhomely moments' and play with the 'contact zones.' In doing so, the Curriculum Spaces notion provides exciting ways to interrupt and to reveal the subaltern subject positions created in this historic moment.

In light of this and other difficult historical moments, I continue to immerse myself in the intellectual journey I have attempted to outline here. It is a very messy journey and I actually enjoy the ambiguity and struggle in opposition. Gilroy (1993) states, "I intend not only to question the credibility of a tidy, holistic conception of modernity but also to argue for the inversion of the relationship between margin and center as it has appeared within the master discourses of the master race." The fluid Self provides a site of resistance. I desire to personalize theory and live between the spaces. According to Gilroy (1993) intellectual exiles (artists, poets, activists, speakers) have articulated "a desire to escape the restrictive bonds of ethnicity, national identification, and sometimes even 'race' itself." Thus, I desire to be such an exile through my work in the academy, as an intellectual working amidst skepticism and sometimes even outright opposition, utilizing discourses and curriculum spaces to expose the obstacles that reduces Self and jails me at 'home' (Gilroy, 1994).

At Home—Theoretically Speaking

However, I cannot conclude a chapter that discusses Curriculum Spaces at the local or subject level without explication of the journey of knowing and the arrivals/departures within that journey. This work is framed by earlier work on notions of home and travel in ethnographic representation (Cary, 1999b). The theories that frame the Curriculum Spaces Research Theory discuss epistemological issues as space, terrain and location (Bhabha, 1994; Foucault, 1977; Spivak, 1995). The issue of location is one of contested terrain, multiple locations and knowing in a state-of-flux. One of the possible outcomes of this theoretical development is to complicate assumptions of site, location, time. It enables us to blur the boundedness of traditional educational research (read here, ethnographic research). As discussed earlier, Clifford (1988, 1992, 1997), Kaplan (1996), Gilroy (1993), Pratt (1992), Dubois (1995) and Bhabha (1994) use a variety of terms to discuss the movement of cultures and the global and local forces that shape them and enhance the kinesthetic quality of culture. As Clifford (1986) states, "'Cultures' do not hold still for their portraits—they are dynamic. Attempts to make them do so always involve simplification and exclusion, selection of a temporal focus, the construction of a partial self-other relationship, and the imposition or negotiation of a power relationship" (p. 10).

As discussed in chapter two, studying culture as motion-filled or asking the question—How does culture travel?—requires a postmodern vision of seemingly improbable juxtapositions. For example, the global collapsed into and made an integral part of parallel, related local situations, rather than being something monolithic and external to them. This move toward comparison as juxtaposition firmly deterritorializes culture in ethnographic writing. It also stimulates accounts of cultures composed in a landscape for which there is as yet no developed theoretical conception (Marcus, 1994, p. 566).

Clifford (1986, 1988, 1992, 1997) has been rather successful in his attempt to reshape the future of ethnographic practice as a focus on 'traveling cultures.' He has attempted to carve out the discipline in order to dismiss the 'poorer' practices and redeem the pure and academic 'travel' practice. Although this is a political and problematic move it has supplied some very useful ideas. Motion, home and knowledge production are all part of Clifford's conceptualization of travel:

> Travel, as I use it, is an inclusive term embracing a range of more or less voluntarist practices of leaving 'home' to go to some 'other' place. This displacement takes place for the purpose of gain—material, spiritual, scientific. It involves obtaining knowledge and/or having an 'experience' (exciting, edifying, pleasurable, estranging, broadening). The long history of travel that includes the spatial practices of 'fieldwork' is predominantly Western-dominated, strongly male, and upper-middle class (Clifford, 1997, p. 66).

Clifford (1997) challenges postmodern ethnographic representations to enhance the cultural performance of space and place. He also presents a counterhegemonic discourse that extends cultural boundaries and highlights the "transgressive intercultural frontiers of nations, peoples, locales. Stasis and purity are asserted—against historical forces of movement and contamination" (Clifford, 1997, p. 7). This is very pertinent to this study as I have attempted to re-represent a number of interconnecting discourses that require a blurring of modernistic boundaries. Clifford (1997) is cognizant of the hegemonic forces at play and thus calls for an inherently partial analysis that works against the essentialist traditions of ethnography. As any term is apt to fail, so Clifford believes that 'travel' fails as a counter-authentic turn in cultural representation or translation as every focus excludes and no methodology or terminology is innocent. "It follows that there is no cure for the troubles of cultural politics in some old or new vision of consensus or universal values. There is only more translation" (Clifford, 1997, p. 13).

The following questions asked by Clifford (1997) have been most useful in the cultural understanding of this project:

> Why not focus on any culture's farthest range of travel while *also* looking at its centers, its villages, its intensive fieldsites? How do groups negotiate themselves in external relationship, and how is a culture also a site of travel

A Postcolonial Subject Position

for others? How are spaces traversed from outside? To what extent is one groups core another's periphery? (Clifford, 1997, p. 25).

Clifford (1997) troubles the assumptions of 'home' and 'travel' by disturbing the dichotomous nature of location and self/other. Traditional ethnographic practices privilege dwelling over travel and in many ways conceptualizing home has been a challenge to the centering of fieldwork or travel as the successor of fieldwork in ethnography (Visweswaran, 1994; Dubois, 1995; Bhabha, 1994; Kaplan, 1996). Home, or dwelling, is not the new ethnography's center. It is, according to Visweswaran (1994), 'deterritorialization' and displacement that are being valorized by some as a mode of being and an imaginative act. Home, however, may be seen as a site of resistance within colonization:

> Uncritically theorized notions of deterritorialization project too comprehensively a 'global homelessness' and displacement, trivializing the political particularities of the phenomenon and erasing the 'resolutely local' homesites necessary both for First World anthropologists to interrogate their own privilege and for less privileged subjects to claim home as a place of nurturance and protection. Is it a coincidence, then, that while many feminist theorists identify home as the site of theory, male critics write to eradicate it? (Visweswaran, 1994, p. 111).

Dubois (1995) describes the quest of anthropology as the mystical common experience of estrangement, homesickness, homelessness, and homeness—"there's the invisible core of what we do, the place we'll always have to come home to, no matter what" (Dubois, 1995, p. 306). In this light the quest for knowledge and cultural understanding is seen blurred as always already travel and always already home. Bhabha (1994) highlights the possibility of going 'beyond' establishing boundaries in order to wonder about home and the world, as unhomed not homeless. I have discussed this previously in chapters one and two.

Bhabha (1994) and Ong (1995) use the concept of home also as a site for feminist resistance against the patriarchal and gendered nature of social reality. They use it to interrogate the domestic space as normalizing and the personal/public binary as regulatory. They move beyond the romantic notions by developing the concept of the unhomed to create a space for cultural difference. According to Bhabha (1994), "the unhomely moment relates to the traumatic ambivalences of a personal, psychic history to the wider disjunctions of political existence" (p. 11).

And so we end at the beginning of a journey toward understanding how the construction of contested terrain of educational research shapes the way we know. This had bled into the development of a theoretical position that draws heavily upon scholars who focus on space as an epistemological issue and my vulgar move into these spaces as curriculum issues—issues that highlight exclusion and subjectification on the bodies of individuals—teachers as we know them in educational reform, students in charter schools, juvie girls as institutionalized subjects and Alien academics and the travels of my own body—we are not homeless—but we are unhomely.

Postscript

In this chapter I have attempted to be strategic. I presented my 9/11 story and then finished off with a safer discussion—theorizing how I came to think of cultural homes, travel and space at the personal level. I chose this path because when I first began presenting and publishing my personal/professional response to 9/11 I received a variety of responses, ranging from gratitude for presenting a part of the stories of foreign faculty in the United States to a sort of aggressive hyper-nationalistic attack for my approach. It seemed a lot of people thought I should be more grateful for the opportunity to be here—I was often confronted with anger and disgust. So, in this presentation I have attempted to highlight the negotiation aspect of the whole thing and the move beyond oppositional to a more productive questioning. This attention to the detailed theorizing of lived experience is an attempt to remind us of the danger of being comfortable in our academic oppositionality. Such comfort in oppositional spaces has often led to a reinscription of the dominant culture and has not effected change. Therefore, by creating new spaces for discussion and possibilities for other ways of being we are on the right track, but we are also outside the mainstream. However, I am torn—we live in a contradictory and messy time.

So, while I am most appreciative of the opportunities to live and work in the United States and recently successfully completed my negotiation of the immigration process and got my 'Greencard' (aka

A Postcolonial Subject Position

Permanent Resident Card—and not Green…)—I am still the Alien Other and yet privileged by race and language. There is still so much to reveal and so much to think about when it comes to how Curriculum Spaces are framed and negotiated at the local level.

6
The Hollywood Teacher: Knowing through Film

This chapter brings it all together and provides an opportunity for a bit of fun in the process. What follows is a discussion of representations of 'teacher' in film as a ludic strategy to blur the boundaries of the societal, institutional and local subject production of Curriculum Spaces as they emerge in populist representations of knowing. Films are one of the most useful texts of populist discourses. Ellsworth (1997) asks us to remember to consider the question: Who does the film think you are? When we take this question to consider our position as teacher, educational researchers or pre-service teachers we must wonder about the discourses of our professional lives that are textualized and reinscribed in films about teaching, education, or about critical educational issues (such as race, class, gender and sexuality). As such, I present a brief discussion of a number of different films and the varying representations of teacher and education. A number of different films are discussed, starting with an overview of contemporary films and concluding with a discussion of two vintage films—*Goodbye Mr. Chips* and *The Prime of Miss Jean Brodie,* in an effort to interrupt the way we know teachers. Overall, this chapter highlights the ways discursively produced populist thought frames the way we know teachers, or 'what a teacher should be' in filmic representations. The journey of researching these texts is one way to think about the production of the curriculum spaces of being and knowing 'a good teacher.' Fascinating issues of discipline, sexualized knowing, gender and race appear in these seemingly harmless Hollywood representations.

Two major discursive frames have emerged in the previous chapters and are highly relevant here. They are the redemptive nature of social and educational discourses, according to Popkewitz (1998c), and the production of crisis talk in education and in terms of today's 'violent' youth (Michaelis, 1999, Rodriguez, 1997; Acland, 1995, Cary, 2003b). In this chapter I address the characters, plots and settings of a selection of contemporary films that focus on teachers, and education using these two discursive frames—the Curriculum Spaces of redemption and the Curriculum Space of crisis—for organization. These two spaces are not inviolable and blur with multiple points of intersection—but have been artificially separated for strategic purposes.

Redemptive Spaces and Youth in Trouble

The three levels of critical discourse analysis as outlined by Fairclough (1995) and discussed in chapter one focus on the societal, institutional and local knowledges that are discursively produced and that we negotiate in our lives. Our lives as educators blur the professional/personal boundaries of how we know the subject position of teacher. By using films in my undergraduate and graduate classes in the College of Education, I have found a way to bring the students to a space of knowing and wondering about the discourses that have shaped the way they know teachers as iconic representations of the 'good' and virginal individual (and I think that carries over onto male and female subject positions) who wants to save and heal the sick youth of today (or yesterday, if you consider vintage films), whether it is the impressive Principal coming out of retirement to save the school (*Lean on Me*) or the retired military personnel who use all the grit and violence of military life to 'save' the youth in '*Dangerous Minds.*' There are so many notions of what it takes to be a good teacher embedded in such films—as a reflection of the populist knowing of teachers that swirls around us in everyday life. Other discourses are also embedded in such films, especially the discourse of the Other—specifically, race or racialized knowing and raced bodies in the youth in crisis discourse. All too often it is a White teacher who comes to save the students of color. This image is interrupted in films that center teachers or administrators of color—but the youth in crisis, raced and visibly different from hegemonic representations—are still presented in a deficit light.

Of course, heroes and heroines so exist in these representations—conflicted yet dedicated to the profession and to their students. *Dead Poets Society* is a fine example of the inspirational and mystical elements of teaching. However, the trick here in using film is not to be realist in the discussion of who the teacher is in the film and how that connects or disconnects with your image as a preservice teacher or experienced teacher. Rather, the idea here is to reveal the Curriculum Spaces that are produced discursively through the representations of Populist, societal, institutional and local knowledges of that subject position. I have found that the danger of using film in education is the trap of entertainment and exoticism that has become a part of our lives without question. So, you must dig deeper—what knowings of teacher are possible and impossible when seen through the multiple representations we see in the media? What does this tell us about the subject position of teacher? How might we use this knowledge of the 'way we know' teachers to interrupt and complicate the way we know our personal/professional lives? In what ways do these representations equity issues in education, such as exclusion through race, violence by gender, and the erasure of Othered sexualized knowings? In the next section, I step into vintage film as a way to investigate the commonsense assumptions and populist notions of teacher that have shaped teachers in film.

Vintage Films

It is vital to explore the complexities of knowing 'teacher' by means of analysis of the discourses presented in vintage films about a 'teacher'. It builds on previous work on vintage films (Cary and Reifel, 2003; Cary, 2004), and the aim of this work is to consider the implications of studying teacher as simulacra, as a layered, complex actor who is not reduced to the normative, reductive spaces of being a 'teacher' in the current educational/professional climate. This section aims to reveal what it means *Not* to be teacher—what is said and unsaid. The question addressed was: What does it mean to be a 'good' teacher, or a 'bad' and dangerous teacher? And *a la* Ellsworth (1997)—who does the film think you are? In other words—how does the normalized construction of what we know as a 'good teacher' interact with the portrayal of Brodie as teacher in *The Prime of Miss Jean Brodie* or Chips in *Goodbye, Mr. Chips*? And, even more interesting—do I see myself in these characters? Is this a possibility—why and why not?

The concept of a simulacra of teacher has framed this discussion. I use simulacra as a 'useful' way of studying teacher without falling into traditional notions of teacher image. Lather (1991) describes it as a copy without an original drawing on the Baudrillardian argument that there has been a shift from a culture of representations to a culture of simulacra. Thus, when used in this way, the simulacra of teacher highlights how "epistemological insufficiency can generate practices of knowing that put[s] the rationalistic and evidentiary structures of science under suspicion in order to address how science betrays our investment in it" (Lather, 2001c, p 3). Referring to the subject position of 'teacher' in this way makes possible the exploration of the layers of discourse that construct the specific examples in each vintage film text. However, I also wonder about Jean Brodie as an anti-teacher—almost antichrist like—and Chips as Hyper-Teacher. It all comes back to how we know a 'good teacher.'

The questions I ask include—what do we desire as teachers, what are we allowed to desire, and how is desire produced in these texts and in the classroom. In previous work, I have used the notion of desire as one way of studying what it means to be a teacher (Cary, 2001; 2000). The work of Deborah Britzman (1998) and Alice Pitt (1998) was central to this analysis as they suggest a move toward a complicated understanding of research and educational practices and away from a wish for heroism and rescue through research (Lather, 1998). This has been particularly useful for rethinking the representation of 'teacher' in this study as a way to "unseat the authority of the humanist subject by insisting upon the notion of the unconscious" (Pitt, 1998, p. 537). Analyzing the film texts in terms of objects of desire enables a different discussion to take place—a discussion that insists on the role of the unconscious (Pitt, 1998). The previously unexplored aspect of desire in the simulacra of teacher opens up the analysis of the layers of discursive organization as constructing (and deconstructing) ideals of 'good teacher,' 'popular teacher,' 'teacher as friend' and teacher in social relationship' (Foucault, 1977; McWilliam, 1999; Popkewitz, 1998b). In this way we can consider the 'difficult knowledge' of education by exploring the question, status and directionality of interference and the issues of love, hate and transference (Britzman, 1998).

The Perfect Teacher—Mr. Chips

Goodbye, Mr. Chips (1939) is an award-winning film, based on the popular, sentimental novel, 'Good-bye, Mr. Chips' (1934) written by James Hilton. In this section, numbered citations refer directly to the film script (reels and scenes, etc.,) by Sheriff, West and Maschwitz (1939). Hilton apparently based his novel on his own schooling experiences with a teacher who was influential on him. The plot describes the transformation of Mr. Chipping from his earliest days as an incompetent, unpopular novice teacher in an English public school for boys, to his death 58 years later, when he is viewed with respect and affection for his contributions to the school and its boys' lives. The film is framed as a retrospective, a long flashback and we first meet Mr. Chipping as a very old teacher in Brookfield School, a venerable, upper-class boarding school (a very white, very male context). The students have heard that Mr. Chips, as he is fondly nicknamed, is ailing at the start of the new school term however, in spite of his ailment, Chips appears late at the school door, only to be locked out of the first assembly with a new boy. They spend their time chatting, with Chips offering empathic comfort to the new boy until the completion of assembly. At that point, Chips is introduced to a new teacher and invited to reflect with the new teacher on the "secret" of Chips' success as a teacher. Chips provides modest, vague comments on how he was given the "secret" by someone else, as he dodders off to prepare a tea party for returning boys. While waiting for his student guests, Chips drifts off into a nap, where he dreams of his 58 years of teaching and life. The dream is the cinematic flashback that tells us his story.

The film sets up a sacred story about teaching (Craig, 1995). It is the story of a modest but very successful practitioner. Chips moves from a very naive teacher to an accomplished 'master' teacher. Scenes from his first attempts at teaching (with no preservice training beyond a content-area degree in Latin) highlight the lack of control and discipline expected in a classroom setting. It was not 'good teaching' and highlights the complexity of teaching as requiring more than subject or content area expertise. The head of school addresses Chips' failure, not with techniques for managing boys or for guiding a group, but by offering ideals: 'Our profession is not an easy one, Mr. Chipping: it calls for something more than a University degree. Our business is to mold men. It demands character and courage' (Sheriff, West and Maschwitz, 1939, 2, 2, 9A). One of the most interesting and powerful discourses of the film is that the daily activities of teaching are tied to the long-term redemptive and social engineering goals of education. Another related discourse is the production of notions of 'character' and citizenship education, reflecting the discussion presented in chapter two. Issues of teaching as character building, cultural capital, privilege and class knowledge, and heteronormative masculinity are present. Success in teaching is a very interesting element of this vintage film. Early on Chips confesses that he failed to gain a more prestigious teaching position at Harrow. And throughout the film Chips highlights that the aim of the successful teacher should be a move into administration. This reflects Lortie's (1975) research that highlights the notion that teachers who remain in the classroom throughout their careers are seen as less successful. The produces a Curriculum Space that is dated, masculinist and progressivist and that reflects traditional notions of success as an issue domination and money-earning capacity. 'It seems that a 'good teacher' is not worth as much as an administrator, and that 'getting on' in education means leaving the classroom' (Cary and Reifel, 2003, p. 19). The film does interrupt this notion by highlighting the value of Chips' career from novice to expert in the classroom and the value of relationships in teaching. However, in every other way it reinscribes notions of 'teacher as savior' and the vocational aspects of the profession. Chips is a 'good teacher'—one who cares and gives his life for his job.

The Anti-Teacher—Miss Jean Brodie

"She was held in great suspicion" (Spark, 1961, p. 2). Brodie is the antithesis of Chips! The main discourse that frames these texts is the emergence of the anti-teacher, the deviant and dangerous character of Jean Brodie. In this way we are reminded of the discourses of the good—good teacher, good girl, good citizen. Brodie is none of the above. The 'data' for this section is the film text "The Prime of Miss Jean Brodie" and the novel of the same name used as the basis for the film, authored by Muriel Sparks in 1961 (quotes used in this section are taken from the novel).

The presentation of the deviant reaffirms and reinscribes the social constructions of teacher and women even more vociferously than any characterization of a safe and virginal female teacher ever could. The discourses of societal, institutional and local knowing emerge and concretize the notion of teacher. A number of themes emerge, including: the 'nature' of teacher—as charismatic and egocentric; the character of Brodie offering details of her own travel experiences as 'curriculum'; the development of the "Brodie girls" (issues of inclusion and exclusion) as a special cult of students with interests of their own; teacher behavior—for example, Brodie values some student contributions while disparaging others. In this text, clearly the only thing that matters is Brodie's agenda, not the girls or

The Hollywood Teacher

the subject matter. The curriculum is redefined by her agenda. It is an outrageous simulacra of teacher as uncontrolled desire (no self-regulation here) and thus complicates how we construct/know teacher.

> If anyone comes along," said Miss Brodie, "in the course of the following lesson, remember that it is the hour for English grammar. Meantime I will tell you a little of my life when I was younger than I am now, though six years older than the man himself (Spark, 1961, p. 9).

This film reveals a number of layers of discourse that may not appear in more contemporary films. It centers desire. The emphasis in contemporary films on student problems tends to distract from the rich and complicated ways that teachers may relate to students. This provides a way into dangerous and unsaid constructions that highlight normalizing assumptions and reduce the subject position of 'teacher' to a reductive and essentialized position.

Brodie is a 'bad egg'—a dangerous teacher—a bad citizen and a bad girl. She brings sex and desire into the classroom (or reveals it at work—rather than oppressing and erasing the body). She is an inspiration gone wrong.

> At that time they had been immediately recognized as Miss Brodie's pupils, being vastly informed on a lot of subjects irrelevant to the authorized curriculum, as the headmistress said, and useless to the school (Spark, 1961, p. 1).

Besides learning about 'irrelevant content'—one student dies in the civil war in Spain and another is prostituted to Brodie's former lovers. Good grief—death and desire in the classroom!

> Sandy recalled Miss Brodie's admiration for Mussolini's marching troops, and the picture she had brought back from Italy showing the triumphant march of the black uniforms in Rome... It occurred to Sandy, there at the end of the Middle Meadow Walk, that the Brodie set was Miss Brodie's fascisti (Spark, 1961, p. 31).

So many layers of danger and desire in the classroom. The power of the character is in the interruption of the normalized construction of the 'good teacher'—a social, historical and cultural construction—the intersection of the discourses that make the construction of the 'good teacher' the possible subject position and Miss Jean Brodie the 'impossible' subject.

Some of the discourses that frame how we know the 'good teacher' and thus how we know Brodie as an interruption or anti-teacher are:

- the sociohistorical construction of teacher as a gendered subject position—highly feminized;
- Sexualized constructions—virginal teachers and marriage as legitimization;
- Technical rationalist constructions of skills/craft of teaching—behaviorist (developmental);
- Disciplined bodies—of teachers and students—discipline students (the cult of personality with 'Brodie's girls' as favored students); and
- Pleasure in pedagogy (McWilliam, 1999).

> We ought to be doing history at the moment according to time-table. Get out your history books and prop them up in your hands. I shall tell you a little more about Italy and a young poet by a fountain (Spark, 1961, p. 48).

Thus the character of Brodie produces perverse pedagogy, with no evidence of planning or direction (Connelly and Clandinin, 1995). The curriculum becomes corrupted with ideological content (fascism and the cult of personality).

> Miss Brodie has already selected her favorites, or rather those whom she could trust; or rather those whose parents she could trust not to lodge complaints about the more advanced and seditious aspects of her educational policy, these parents being either too enlightened to complain or too unenlightened, or too awed by their good fortune in getting their girls' education at endowed rates, or too trusting to question the value of what their daughters were learning at this school of sound reputation. Miss Brodie's girls were taken home to tea and bidden not to tell the others, they were taken into her confidence, they understood her private life and her feud with the headmistress and the allies of the headmistress (Spark, 1961, p. 25).

In the end, however, the film reproduces the normative notions of the good, virginal teacher by presenting the danger of the Other, the perverted and resistant teacher. The way we know teacher is exoticized through a Curriculum Space of deviant knowledge, for example, the deviant discipline that is used to shape the 'Brodie Girls.'

A Psychoanalytic Moment

Ellsworth's (1997) work has proved most useful to me in teaching about teaching and in using films in undergraduate and graduate education classes to highlight and reveal the way things play out through the social and educational discourses that frame the way we know teaching (Popkewitz, 1998c). *"Teaching Positions: Difference, Pedagogy, and the Power of Address"* has been most useful to me as I consider the question—is teaching possible? (Ellsworth, 1997, p. 55). Is teaching about race, class, gender, ethnicity, etc., possible? She highlights the role of the unconscious and the way in which curriculum (such as films) have intended audiences yet fail to 'produce' sameness, for example, a generically good citizen. There are three participants in pedagogy, according to Ellsworth, the teacher, the student and the unconscious.

Ellsworth (1997) troubles assumptions in education and highlights the realists desire for 'full' understanding and consensus in education is not an innocent endeavor (p. 33). She asks:

> What might a teacher's mode of address be to a student when the teacher is not fully cognizant of her own knowledge, desire, ignorances—and cannot have direct access to the unconscious roots of the student's resistances, miscognitions, and active refusals? (p. 62).

Using her background in Media Studies, Ellsworth discusses modes of address in films as a construction of reality that makes assumptions about who the audience is. Therefore, the question is—who does the film-maker think you are? Transferring this question to address education, Ellsworth complicates the concept of pedagogical address as deeply personal and meaningful when she says that "dialogue is not a neutral vehicle. It has a particular job in mind" (p. 49).

Ellsworth outlines the failed promise of education as the assuming that communicative dialogue is a neutral conduit of reality, and she describes the persuasive nature of this 'neutral' conduit as follows:

> Dialogue in education is assumed to be capable of everything from constructing knowledge to resolving problems, to ensuring democracy, to securing understanding, to teaching, to alleviating racism or sexism, to arriving at ethical and moral claims, to enacting our humanity, to fostering community and connection (p. 85).

There is nothing neutral or natural about Brodie.

Ellsworth uses the idea of cultivating a 'third ear' in preservice teachers to enable them to listen "not for what the student knows (discrete packages of knowledge) but for the terms that shape a student's knowing, her not knowing, her forgetting, her circles of stuck places and resistances" (p. 70). The questions she highlights as vital for teacher education could also be used for graduate study in educational research and related issues of curriculum discourses. For example:

- What happens to my process of thinking, my own symbolic constellation when I read this author's words?
- Where, as I read this author, do I get stuck, do I forget, do I resist?
- Where, when I listen to a classmate's response to this reading, does my own project of 'becoming a teacher' [or researcher] get shifted, troubled, unsettled—why there? Why now?

Ellsworth (1997) asks us to picture a teacher education program, (and I add here—a graduate curriculum studies program or an educational research program) 'founded' on the undecidability of teaching, on the interminable process of reading as a teacher. Her use of Magical Realism encourages one to ask—"What's counting as real here? What's counting as unreal, excessive, distorted? Who's counting it as real and why?" (p. 179). By highlighting the unconscious, Ellsworth is one of an increasing number of educational theorists utilizing psychoanalysis as a way of addressing paradoxes in education. In the case of Brodie, the anti-teacher revels in these paradoxes. The following paradoxes with/in pedagogy are central to Ellsworth's (1997) work:

- The paradox of social agency, as in the taking of action that is affirmative without positive reference, without knowing what good the action will do;
- The paradox of authority and power in the pedagogical

relation;
- The paradox of the pedagogical event, which leaves no *visible* trace of its happening;
- The paradox of pedagogy as performative—as a taking of action that is, nevertheless, always suspended in the space between self and other; and,
- The paradox of pedagogy as a performative act that is always suspended in the undecidable time of learning (p. 142).

The paradoxes outlined above are important to include in any 'dialogue' in preservice or graduate education classrooms as one way to attempt to avoid the temptations of realist tales and to also avoid the comfort of essentialist or reductive socially constructed knowing.

So What?

But what shall we do with this? Rather than avoid the undecidability and uncertainty, the deviant and the canonical, I think we should embrace it. We can learn so much about our self-regulated professional and personal lives through understanding such Curriculum Spaces and this, in turn, might lead to increased possibilities for interruption. We should embrace the stories of Mary Kay Le Torneau and others to teach us about our discursively produced and framed knowing. Dangerous knowledge can be very useful in preservice teacher education and in graduate classrooms. My previous work on citizenship as constructed in teacher education reform (see chapter two) highlights the historical feminized caring and kind teacher. Jean Brodie is none of those things. She is an outcast sent to teach us about teachers. Why is she so powerful? So dangerous? So deviant? She refuses (or Sparks refuses, or Maggie Smith refuses...) the construction and thus interrupts the normalized subject position. She looks the part—but that could be due to the familiarity you will find with accepted notions of the 'good teacher.'

Where is the capacity to tolerate learning in the construction of the 'good teacher' The call for technical rationalist mastery is a push to control. It sets in motion a number of forms of anxiety that "render unthinkable the chance to understand without recourse to mastery" (Britzman, 1998, 26). Just as current educational reform discourses of 'reflective practice' and 'critical thinking' valorize mastery and the quest for rationality, so does the construction of the 'good teacher.' It promotes the mastery of technical competence that ignores the im/possibilities of learning by reducing teaching to simplistic representations. According to Britzman (1998), anything else is seen as an irrelevancy, off-the-point, off-the-subject, and a waste of time. Excellence, expertise and competence are the 'stories' or dreams (central themes) of the Curriculum Spaces surrounding and legitimizing the good teacher. However, any call for a cure or mastery is a failure. There is no redemptive or rescue fantasy out there—nor in this text. One loses the elusive subject in the question of redemption: "The paradox is that learning is provoked in the failure to learn" (Britzman, 1998, p. 31). The question instead is: "Can education be a place where thoughts not only are troubled but are troubled to explore how our thoughts get us in and out of trouble?" (Britzman, 1998, p. 32).

The dream of public education—or the dream of the 'good teacher'—the object of desire—seems to be one of progress and mastery. It implies a 'forgetting' of the conflict it requires. The discursive production of the 'good teacher' is an effect of educational design (or a Foucauldian technology of power) (Britzman, 1998). I suggest here that anxiety becomes 'the curriculum' as the trauma of education is its inability to come to terms with its own conflicted history: "There is then, in all of this life, a fundamental contradiction that makes the project of education inconsolable" (Britzman, 1998, p. 55). How may we refigure the construction of teacher in the text of the film as desire gone awry—by refusing the simple and moralistic romance of teacher education (Britzman, 1998; Lather, 1998; McCoy, 1995)? By being interested in the mistakes, the accidents, the detours and unintelligibilities of identities? Without guarantees, the "responsibility for fashioning new meanings, for making new projects, lies elsewhere: in the doing of dialogue, in the arguments over what can constitute authenticity, appropriation and the limits of culture in the *bildungsroman* community/commonalities] of schooling" (Britzman, 1998, p. 60).

7
From Currere to Curriculum Spaces

This chapter, specifically, and the book in general, respond to Morrison's (2004) call for new curriculum theory. Therefore, by drawing on a variety of scholars I situate this chapter within the larger scene of the curriculum field and debates of the last decade (Morrison, 2004; Graham, 1992; Short, 1991; Reynolds and Webber, 2004; Pinar, 2004). As previously mentioned, Morrison (2004) in an article entitled, "The Poverty of Curriculum Theory: a Critique of Wraga and Hlebowitsh" addressed the need for new, open-ended curriculum theories that moved beyond the historically inscribed limitations outlined again and again by Wraga and Hlebowitsh.

> Recycling ideas leads to curriculum closure; it goes nowhere. Novelty and originality are required to move forward the fields of curriculum theory and development. However one may wish to package it, the message is the same: move on; discover and invent new worlds and new ideas (Morrison, 2004, p. 487).

This is an important moment for curriculum theory if it is to move beyond not only traditional prescriptions as outlined by Morrison (2004) but also if it is to move beyond Pinar and Grumet's (1976) interpretivist approach, *Currere*, which both opened and closed the reconceptualized field of curriculum to the study of gestalt over the last decades. This piece is a response to this call that opens up a space for other ways of understanding curriculum. The role that Pinar and Grumet (1976) played was a vital one and Currere as a curriculum theory was strong enough to have the potential to move the curriculum debate forward. Graham (1992) highlights the paradigm or generational shift that possibly occurred in the wake of currere:

> And yet it is extremely likely that, in typical Kuhnian fashion, a new generation of scholars sympathetic to reconceptualist thinking is slowly in the process of coming into its own. If this is so, it may signify that, for a significant number of workers in curriculum, reconceptualism still represents one of the best hopes for keeping the human factor alive in education, especially at a time of widespread political retrenchment, a global movement whose impetus at present shows few signs of exhaustion (Graham, 1992, p. 40).

Now it is time to present theories that emerged from other paradigms and in this case, from the postmodern/deconstructivist paradigm. It is, as Morrison (2004) suggests, time to abandon any grand unified theory (traditionalist or reconceptualist) and celebrate the difficult and uncomfortable field that may result. However, this call to new theory is not without guidelines: "Rather, a 'good' theory in education, as Cohen et al (2000) remark, gathers together all the isolated pieces of data into a coherent conceptual framework of wider applicability; it comprises a set of inter-related constructs, definitions, and propositions that presents a systematic view of phenomena, and moves thinking forward into new vistas" (Morrison, 2004, p. 488). Recently, Pinar (2004) also called for this widening of the field:

> Rejecting colonization by the hegemonic disciplines such as psychology, curriculum theory explores and constructs hybrid interdisciplinary constructions, utilizing fragments from philosophy, history, literary theory, the arts, and from those key interdisciplinary formations already in place: women's and gender studies, African-American studies, queer theory, studies in popular culture, among others... In drawing—promiscuously but critically—from various academic disciplines and popular culture, curriculum theorists work to create conceptual montages for the public-school teacher who understands that positionality as aspiring to create a 'public' space (p. 33).

Curriculum Spaces Research Theory attempts to do just that. This works reflects an epistemological crisis that draws upon poststructural, postcolonial and psychoanalytic theories to lead us beyond static understandings of how we know, to more fluid and complicated knowledge that reveals exclusions and objectifications at work in educational settings. This is a move for more accessible theorizing in Curriculum Studies as an ethical responsibility in these historically inscribed times.

The second layer of this piece outlines the importance of connecting curriculum theory and educational research. It is a curriculum issue and emerged in response to Pinar's (2004) call for a more complicated conversation that centers interdisciplinary intellectuality, erudition and self-reflexivity. Therefore, this curriculum theory centers knowing and spaces of knowing as a discursive production that shapes the educational experience on all levels. This centering of epistemological spaces (theories of knowing) the ontologically (the nature of the real) impacts the lives of Others. This strategic use of language highlights that *the way we know what we know* is a curriculum issue—a Curriculum Space. It is an ethical turn toward responsibility in research and away from simply theoretical meanderings (St. Pierre, 2000). This is a response to the call for engagement with specific complex problems in curriculum that do not have generalizable solutions (St. Pierre, 2000).

Short (1991) and Reynolds and Webber (2004) also connected research or inquiry to the curriculum field. However, in both cases what emerged was a presentation of different methodological approaches (or, as Short called them, inquiries) rather than a discussion of foundational research theory or issues. The presentation of Curriculum Spaces presented here is situated within a number of major research issues and claims the notion of research, not inquiry, as a more rigorous position. In this way, curriculum scholars might connect with the larger research community as 'researchers,' rather than the softer and less valid signification of inquiry. Historically this move to name inquiry might be seen as a strategic one to break the hold of traditional positivist/objectivist as the only legitimate approach to curriculum study. That move, and the paradigm wars in the field, as Short (1991) suggests, is a past debate and it should not be required any longer as "the battle of the 1970's and 1980's waged within the field of curriculum studies over introducing some of the newer forms of curriculum inquiry are for the most part behind us and that now more careful and balanced discourse, with less political and polemic overtones, is the order of the day in the 1990's" (Short, 1991, p. 333). Rather, it is time to claim research in all paradigms and to complicate our understanding of curriculum.

The field of educational research will also benefit greatly from this discussion because it is time to do more than merely position the researcher in qualitative research. Lather (2004) states that it is time for a "turn toward more concrete efforts to put theory to work" (p. 2). It is time to call upon educational researchers to work to understand that the way they know what they know also impacts the lives of those they study, research and teach. This is a discursive and recursive relationship (Foucault, 1977; Jagodzinski, 2002). It is an ethical turn that has emerged from the linguistic turn. It is a 'making sense' of difficult knowledge and reflects the crisis of representation (Clifford, 1986).

Where Do We Go From Here?

Curriculum Spaces Research Theory is a 'vulgar' approach. This is because it draws upon other theories to build a new way of looking at curriculum, at schooling and at education. Historically, the notion of curriculum space was one of physical space—the classroom, the desk, the school building, the school district, state and nation. Today, I am able to think differently about curriculum because some leading scholars in the field have reconceptualized what 'curriculum' means. Pinar et al. (1995) highlight this turn toward a more complicated understanding of curriculum. This reflects the move from curriculum development to an investigation of the frames that influence education on all levels (Marsh and Willis, 1999). Indeed, it is a move from development to understanding. And with this move, we have begun to wonder about curriculum as lived experience, autobiography, and biography, among other ideas. This book takes understanding curriculum to a new place, the next level (although we don't want to be linear about this, do we?).

Curriculum Spaces Research Theory, as presented here, however, suggests that we may benefit from studying the way we are epistemologically situated as subjects by historical, social and cultural discourses. It is two-fold. First, it is the investigation of epistemological spaces—the study of how we know what we know. This turn toward the individual has focused the study of curriculum on subjectivities—the experiences and social constructions of individuals. This interested me in the way we know, the way we exclude through knowing and the possibilities and impossibilities in these ways of knowing. I began situating my investigation at the level of the multiple subjectivities (or ways of knowing) created, framed, and developed in curriculum. Second, I add to the discussion by suggesting we can understand how the spaces we inhabit are made possible (and impossible) by analyzing the discourses that legitimize these ways of knowing. So, Curriculum Spaces calls for the study of discursive practices to further understand how we know what we know and who we know in educational experiences and in knowing in general (St. Pierre, 2000; Pillow, 2000). It also demands attention to investigating and understanding the fact that knowing shapes and impacts the lives of those we know.

> Curriculum as a governing practice becomes almost self-evident as we think of the 'making' of the proper citizen. This citizen is one who has the correct

dispositions, sensitivities and awareness to act as a self-governing individual in the new political, cultural and economic contexts. Current reforms that focus on 'constructivist pedagogy' and teacher education reforms that considered the 'beliefs' and dispositions' of the teacher are the secularization of the confessional systems of self discipline and control (Popkewitz, 1998c, p. 89).

Ethics

The field of Curriculum Studies, and Curriculum Theory, in particular, according to Pinar (2004), consists of the interdisciplinary study of educational experiences. In this book, therefore, I use the vulgar approach of Curriculum Spaces that draws upon a number of interdisciplinary theories to highlight the move to the study of the knowing subject, the study of epistemology, as framed by social, historical and political discourses (to name a few). It is a chance to step back from this inscribed historical moment of high-stakes testing and accountability, from the politics of terror and global environmental concerns. It is an ethical move to center and reveal how we know in order to act responsibly as informed educators and as informed global citizens. "In our time, to be intellectual requires political activism" (Pinar, 2004, p. 10). Pinar also highlights the "significance of subjectivity" (p. 4), in the process of education, as inseparable from the social. Studying the individual knowing subject is embedded within and against the social.

> The complicated conversation that is the curriculum requires interdisciplinary intellectuality, erudition, and self-reflexivity. This is not a recipe for high test scores, but a common faith in the possibility of self-realization and democratization, twin projects of social and subjective reconstruction (Pinar, 2004, p. 8).

Slattery and Rapp (2003) also address this issue when they center ethical concerns in curriculum work or theorizing. They state: "Ethics cannot be separated from our autobiographical journey or from aesthetics. The complexity of our lives makes the study of critical ethical issues and education an imprecise science at best. However, the process of struggling to understand the complexity of our lives is for us the beginning of wisdom" (p. 67). Thus, I have attempted to engage in a more complicated journey. As a result, this work is a strategically linguistic and ethical turn toward the study of discourses that frame our knowing and the way we know Others.

Bibliography

Abdal-Haqq, Ismat. (1998). *Professional Development Schools: Weighing the Evidence*. Thousand Oaks, California: Corwin Press.

Acland, Charles. (1995). *Youth, Murder, Spectacle: The Cultural Politics of 'Youth in Crisis.'* Boulder, Colorado: Westview Press.

Adams, N. (1997). Feminist poststructuralism and the possibilities of theory in transforming middle level teacher education programs. *Teacher Education Quarterly*, Fall 1997, pp. 117–128.

Adler, Freda. (1975). *Sisters in Crime: The Rise of the New Female Criminal*. New York, New York; McGraw-Hill.

Ageton, Suzanne S. (1983). "The Dynamics of Female Delinquency, 1976–1980." *Criminology*, Volume 21, Number 4, November 1983, pp. 555–584.

Anderson, G. (1998) Toward authentic participation: Deconstructing the discourses of participatory reforms in education. *American Educational Research Journal*, Volume 35, Number 4, pp. 571–603.

Apple, M. W. (1996). *Cultural Politics and Education*. New York: Teachers College Press.

Apple, M. W.and H. St. Maurice. (1991). Social Studies Education and Theory: Science, Knowledge, and History. In J. P. Shaver (ed.), *Handbook of Research on Social Studies Teaching and Learning*. (New York, New York: Macmillan), 27–40.

Archival text 1
Archival text 2
Archival text 3
Archival text 4

Barone, Thomas. (1995). Persuasive Writings, Vigiliant Readings, and Reconstructed Characters: The Paradox of Trust in Educational Storysharing. In Amos J. Hatch and Richard Wisniewski, *Life History and Narrative*. (Washington, DC; Falmer Press), 63–74.

Behar, Ruth. (1995). Introduction: Out of Exile. In Behar, Ruth, and Deborah A. Gordon, *Women Writing Culture*. (Berkeley, California: University of California Press), 1–29.

Berger, Ronald, J. (1989). "Female Delinquency in the Emancipation Era: A Review of the Literature." *Sex Roles*, Volume 21, Numbers 5/6, 1989, pp. 375–399.

Berliner, D. C. (2002). Educational Research: The Hardest Science of All. *Educational Researcher*, Volume 31, Number 8; pp. 18–20.

Bernasconi, R. (1993). Politics beyond Humanism: Mandela and the Struggle Against Apartheid. In G. B. Madison, *Working Through Derrida*. (Evanston, Illinois: Northwestern University Press), 94–121.

Bhabha, Homi K., (1994). *The Location of Culture*. New York, New York: Routledge.

Bjorkqvist, Kaj. (1994). "Sex Differences in Physical, Verbal, and Indirect Aggression: A Review of Recent Research." *Sex Roles*, Volume 30, Numbers 3 and 4; pp. 177–188.

Blumenfeld-Jones. Donald. (1995). Fidelity as a Criterion for Practicing and Evaluating Narrative Inquiry. In Amos J. Hatch and Richard Wisniewski, *Life History and Narrative*. (Washington, DC; Falmer Press), 25–36.

Britzman, Deborah P. (1998). *Lost Subjects, Contested Objects: Toward A Psychoanalytic Inquiry of Learning*. New York, New York: State University of New York Press.

────── (2003). *After-Education: Anna Freud, Melanie Klein, and Psychoanalytic Histories of Learning*. New York, New York; SUNY.

Calhoun, George, Janelle Jurgens and Fengling Chen (1993). "The Neophyte Female Delinquent: A Review of the Literature." *Adolescence*, Volume 28, Number 110, Summer 1993; pp. 461–471.

Canaan, J.E., and Epstein, D. (1997). *A question of discipline: Pedagogy, power, and the teaching of cultural studies*. Boulder, Colorado: Westview Press.

Cary, Lisa. J. (2004). The Prime of Miss Jean Brodie: Desire on the Classroom! *The American Educational Research Association Annual Meeting (AERA)*, San Diego, California.

────── (2003a). In-between curriculum spaces: The effects of power in a post 9/11 world. *The Journal of Curriculum Theorizing*, Volume 19, Number 3; pp. 85–95.

────── (2003b). Unhomely Spaces and Deviant Subjectivity: The Socio-Historical Homelessness of Female Juvenile Offenders. *The International Journal of Qualitative Studies in Education*, Volume 16, Number 4; pp. 579–594.

────── (2001). The Refusals of Citizenship. *Theory and Research in Social Education*. Volume 29, Number 3, Summer 2001; pp. 405–430.

────── (2000). Redemption, Desire and Discourse: The UnApparent Teacher in Education. Conference Proceedings, *The Internationalization of Curriculum Studies Conference*, April 27–30, 2000, Baton Rouge, Louisiana. Http://asterix.ednet.lsu.edu/~lsuctp /2000.htm#anchor75820.

────── (1999a). Unexpected Stories: Life History and the Limits of Representation. *Qualitative Inquiry*, Volume 5 Number 3, 1999; pp. 411–427.

────── (1999b). *Complicating the professional development school: Redemption, desire and discourse*. Unpublished Doctoral Dissertation, The Ohio State University; Columbus, Ohio.

Cary, L.J. and Reifel, S. (2003). Complicating Our Understanding: Teacher as Simulacra in Vintage Film Text. *American Educational Research Association (AERA) 2003 Annual Conference*, Chicago, Illinois.

Casey, K. (1993). *I answer with my life: Life histories of women teachers working for social change*. New York, New York: Routledge.

Chase, Sue and Merry Merryfield. (1998). After the Honeymoon is Over: What Seven Years of Collaboration Have Taught us About School/University Collaboration in Social Studies and Global Education. In Johnston et al (1998 Draft) *Collaborative Reform and other Improbable Dreams: Professional Development Schools at the Ohio State University*. (Columbus, Ohio: The Ohio State University), pp. 124–146.

Chesney-Lind, Meda (1989). "Girls' Crime and Woman's Place: Toward a Feminist Model of Female Delinquency." *Crime and Delinquency*, Volume 35, Number 1, January 1989, pp. 5–29.

Chesney-Lind, Meda and Marliyn Brown (1999). Girls and Violence: An Overview. In Daniel J. Flannery and C. Ronald Huff (eds.), *Youth Violence: Prevention, Intervention, and Social Policy*. (Washington, D.C.: American Psychiatric Press), pp. 171–199.

Chomsky, Noam. (2001). *9/11*. New York, New York; Open Media.

Bibliography

Clandinin, D.J., and Connnelly, F.M. 1995. *Teachers professional knowledge landscapes.* New York, New York: Teachers College Press.

Clifford, James. (1997). *Routes: Travel and Translation in the Late Twentieth Century.* Cambridge, Massachusetts: Harvard University Press.

―――― (1992). Traveling Cultures. In Lawrence Grossberg et al., *Cultural Studies.* (New York, New York: Routledge), pp. 96–112.

―――― (1988). *The Predicament of Culture: Twentieth Century Ethnography, Literature, and Art.* Cambridge, Massachusetts: Harvard University Press.

―――― (1986). Introduction: Partial Truths. In Clifford, James and George E. Marcus (Eds.), *Writing Culture: The Poetics and Politics of Ethnography.* (Berkeley, California: University of California Press), pp. 1–26.

Clifford, J. and Marcus, G. E. (Eds.). (1986). *Writing Culture: The Poetics and Politics of Ethnography.* Berkeley, California: University of California Press.

Cochran-Smith, M. and Lytle, S.L. (1998) Teacher Research: the Question that Persists. *The International Journal of Leadership in Education,* 1 (1), 19–36.

Collins, P. H (1991). *Black Feminist Thought: Knowledge, Consciousness and the politics of Empowerment.* New York: Routlege.

Connelly, F.M., & Clandinin, D.J. (1996). Practice: An analysis. In J. Chafel & S. Reifel (Eds.), *Advances in Early Education and Day Care (vol. 8): Theory and Practice in Early Childhood Teaching* (pp. 91–116). Greenwich, Connecticut: JAI Press.

―――― (1988). *Teachers as curriculum planners: Narratives of experience.* New York: Teachers College Press.

Constas, M. A. (1998). Deciphering postmodern educational research. *Educational Researcher,* 27(9), 36–42.

Craig, Cheryl J. (2001) The Relationships Between and Among Teachers' Narrative Knowledge, Communities of Knowing, and School Reform: A Case of 'The Monkey's Paw'. *Curriculum Inquiry. Volume* 31, Number 3; pp. 303–331.

―――― (2000). Stories of schools/teachers stories: A two-part invention on the walls theme. *Curriculum Inquiry.* Volume 30, Number 1; pp. 11–41.

―――― (1995). Safe Places on the Landscape: Knowledge communities. In D. Jean Clandinin and F. Michael Connelly (Eds.), *Teachers professional knowledge landscapes.* New York, New York: Teachers College Press.

Cramer, D., D. Shinew, and N. Zimpher. (Unpublished Paper). *An historical overview of professional development schools at The Ohio State University.*

Crotty, M. (1998). The Foundations of Social Research: Meaning and Perspective in the Research Process (Thousand Oaks, California; Sage).

Curran, Daniel J. (1984) "The Myth of the 'New' Female Delinquent." *Crime and Delinquency,* Volume 30, Number 3, July 1984; pp. 386–399.

Davies, J.S and Adams, N.G. (2000). Exploring Early Adolescent Identity Through Teacher Autobiography. *Middle School Journal.* January 2000;18–25.

DeCuir, J. T. and Dixson, A. D. (2004). "So, When It Comes Out, They Aren't That Surprised That It Is There": Using Critical Race Theory as a Tool of Analysis of Race and Racism in Education. *Educational Researcher,* Volume 33, Number 5; pp. 26–31.

Delgado, R. (1999). "Citizenship." In R. D. Torres, L. F. Miron, & J. X. Inda (Eds.), *Race, identity, and citizenship: A reader.* (Malden, Massachusetts: Blackwell), pp. 247–252.

Denzin, Norman K. (1994). The Art and Politics of Interpretation. In Norman K. Denzin and Yvonna S. Lincoln (Eds.), *The Handbook of Qualitative Research*. (Thousand Oaks, California; Sage Publications), pp. 500–515.

Donnelly, J. 2002. *Career development for teachers*. Stirling, Virginia: Stylus Publications.

Dubois, Laurent (1995). 'Man's Darkest Hours': Maleness, Travel, and Anthropology. In Ruth Behar and Deborah A. Gordon (Eds.), *Women Writing Culture*. (Berkeley, CA; University of California Press), pp. 306–321.

Eisenhart, M. (1995). The Fax, the Jazz Player, and the Self-Story Teller: How Do People Organize Culture? *Anthropology and Education Quarterly*. Volume 26, Number 1; pp. 3–26.

Ellsworth, Elizabeth (1997). *Teaching Positions: Difference, Pedagogy and the Power of Address*. New York, New York; Teachers College Press.

Ellsworth, Elizabeth (1989). Why Doesn't this Feel Empowering? *Harvard Educational Review*, Volume 59, Number 3; pp. 297-324.

Erickson, F. and Gutierrez, K. (2002). Culture, Rigor, and Science in Educational Research. *Educational Researcher*, 31(8), 21–24.

Fairclough, Norman. (1995). *Critical Discourse Analysis: The Critical Study of Language*. New York, NY: Longman.

Fazzaro, C.J. and Walter, J.E. (2002). Schools for Democracy: Lyotard, dissensus and educational policy. *The International Journal of Leadership in Education*. Volume 5, Number 1; pp. 15–32.

Finn, C. E., Manno, B. V., and Vanourek, G. (2000). *Renewing Public Education: Charter Schools in Action*. Princeton, New Jersey: Princeton University Press.

Foucault, M. (1991). Governmentality. In G. Burchell, C. Gordon, & P. Miller (Eds.), *The Foucault effect: Studies in governmentality*. (Chicago, Illinois: University of Chicago Press), pp. 87–104.

———— (1980). *Power/Knowledge: Selected Interviews and Other Writings, 1972–1977*. Edited by Colin Gordon. New York, New York: Pantheon Books.

———— (1977). *Discipline and Punish*. Translated from French by Alan Sheridan. New York, New York: Vintage Books.

Frankenberg, R. (1993). *White women, race matters: The social construction of whiteness*. Minneapolis: University of Minnesota Press.

Franklin, J. H. (1993). *The color line: Legacy for the twenty-first century*. Columbia: University of Missouri Press.

Frost, J., Wortham, S., and Reifel, S. 2005. *Play and child development*, Second Edition. Columbus, Ohio: Merrill/Prentice Hall.

Fry, Douglas P., and Ayala H. Gabriel (1994). Preface: The Cultural Construction of Gender and Aggression. *Sex Roles*, Volume 30, Numbers 3 and 4, 1994; pp. 165–167.

Fullan, Michael, Gary Galluzzo, Patricia Morris, and Nancy Watson. (1998). *The Rise and Stall of Teacher Education Reform*. Washington, DC.; The American Association of Colleges for Teacher Education.

Gavey, Nicola. (1997). Feminist Poststructuralism and Discourse Analysis. In Mary M. Gergen and Sara N. Davis (eds.), *Toward a New Psychology of Gender: A Reader*. (New York, New York; Routledge), pp. 49-64.

Geertz, Clifford. (1983). *Local Knowledge: Further Essays in Interpretive Anthropology*. New York, NY: Basic Books.

Bibliography

Gilroy, Paul. (1993). *The Black Atlantic: Modernity and Double Consciousness.* Cambridge, Massachusetts: Harvard University Press.

Giroux, H. (2002). Democracy, Freedom, and Justice after September 11th: Rethinking the Role of Educators and the Politics of Schooling. *Teachers College Record Online.*

Goldson, Barry. (1997). Children in Trouble: State Responses to Juvenile Crime. In Scraton, Phil (Ed.) (1997). *'Childhood' in 'Crisis'?* Bristol. Pennsylvania; University College of London Press.

Goodlad, J.I. (Ed.). (1979). *Curriculum inquiry: The study of curriculum practice.* New York: McGraw-Hill.

Goodman, Jesse. (1995). Working with Teachers to Reform Schools: Issues of Power, Expertise and Commitment. In John Smyth, (ed.), *Critical Discourses on Teacher Development.* (New York, New York: Cassell), pp. 65–79.

Goodson, I.F. (1995). The Story so Far: Personal Knowledge and the Political. In Amos J. Hatch and Richard Wisniewski, *Life History and Narrative.* Washington, DC; Falmer Press. 89–98.

―――― (ed.). (1992). *Studying Teacher's Lives.* New York: Teachers College Press.

―――― (1998). Storying the Self: life Politics and the Study of Teacher's Life and Work. In William F. Pinar's (ed.), *Curriculum: Toward New Identities.* (New York, NY; Garland), pp. 3–20.

Graham, Robert J., (1992). Currere and Reconceptualism: the Progress of the Pilgrimage 1975—1990. *The Journal of Curriculum Studies,* 24 (1), 27–42.

Greene, Maxine. (1995*). Releasing the Imagination: Essays on Education, the Arts, and Social Change.* San Francisco, California; Jossey-Bass.

―――― (1994). Epistemology and Educational Research: The Influence of Recent Approaches to Knowledge. In Linda Darling-Hammond (ed.)., *Review of Research in Education.* (Washington, DC.; American Educational Research Association), pp. 423–464.

Harding, S. (Ed.) (1987). *Feminism and methodology.* Bloomington, Indiana: Indiana University Press.

Hartigan, J. (1999). Establishing the fact of whiteness. In R. D. Torres, L. F. Miron, & J. X. Inda (Eds.), *Race, identity, and citizenship: A reader.* (Malden, Massachusetts: Blackwell), pp. 183–199.

Hatch, Amos J. and Wisniewski, Richard. (1995). Life History and Narrative: Questions, Issues and Exemplary Works. In Amos J. Hatch and Richard Wisniewski, *Life History and Narrative.* (Washington, DC: Falmer Press), pp. 113–136.

Heath, D.H. (1994). *Schools of hope: Developing mind and character in today's youth*. San Francisco, California: Jossey-Bass.

Hilton, J. (1934). *Good-bye, Mr. Chips.* Boston, Massachusetts: Little Brown.

Holland, P. E. and Adams, P. (2002). Through the horns of a dilemma between instructional supervision and the summative evaluation of teaching. *The International Journal of Leadership in Education.* Volume 5, Number 3: pp. 227–247.

Holmes Group, The. (1995). *Tomorrow's schools of education.* East Lansing, Michigan: The Holmes Group, Inc.

―――― (1990). *Tomorrow's schools: Principles for the design of professional development schools*. East Lansing, Michigan: The Holmes Group, Inc.

———— (1986). *Tomorrow's Teachers*. East Lansing, Michigan: The Holmes Group, Inc.

hooks, b. (1996). Choosing the Margin as a Space for Radical Openness. In Ann Garry and Marilyn Pearsall (eds.), *Women, Knowledge and Reality: Explorations in Feminist Philosophy*. (New York, New York; Routledge), pp. 48–55.

———— (1994). *Teaching to Transgress: Education as the Practice of Freedom*. New York, New York: Routledge.

———— (1992). *Black Looks: Race and Representation*. Boston, Massachusetts.; South End Press.

———— (1989). *Talking Back: Thinking Feminist, Thinking Black*. Boston, Massachusetts: South End Press.

Hwu, Wen-Song. (1998). Curriclum, Transcendence, and Zen/Taoism: Critical Ontology of the Self. In William F. Pinar (Ed.), *Curriculum: Towards New Identities*. (New York, New York; Garland), pp. 21–40.

Jagodzinski, J. (2002). The Ethics of the "Real" In Levinas, Lacan, and Buddhism: Pedagogical Implications. *Educational Theory*, 52(1), 81–96.

Johnston, Marilyn. (1998). Introduction: Contexts, Challenges, and Consequences: PDSs in the Making. In Johnston et at (1998), *Collaborative Reform and other Improbable Dreams: Professional Development Schools at the Ohio State University*. Draft. (Columbus, Ohio: The Ohio State University), pp. x–xxx.

Johnston, Marilyn, Patti Brosnan, Don Cramer, and Tim Dove (eds.). (1998). *Collaborative Reform and other Improbable Dreams: Professional Development Schools at the Ohio State University*. Draft. Columbus, Ohio: The Ohio State University.

Justice By Gender: The lack of appropriate prevention, diversion and treatment alternatives for girls in the justice system (author). (May 1, 2001). Jointly issued by the American Bar Association and the National Bar Association.

Kaplan, Caren. (1996). *Questions of Travel: Postmodern Discourses of Displacement*. Durham, North Carolina: Duke University Press.

Katz, Susan R. (1997). Presumed Guilty: How Schools Criminalize Latino Youth. *Social Justice*, Winter 1997, Volume 24, Number 4: pp. 77–95.

Koppich, J., Asher, C., and Kerchner, C. 2002. *Developing careers, building a profession: The Rochester career in teaching plan*. New York: National Commission on Teaching & America's Future, (ERIC Doc. # ED472182).

Labaree, David. (1996). The Trouble with Ed Schools. *Educational Foundations*, Summer, 1996: pp. 27–45.

———— (1995). A Disabling Vision: Rhetoric and Reality in *Tomorrow's Schools of Education*. *Teachers College Record*. Volume 97, Number 2. Winter 1995: pp. 166–205

———— (1992). Power, Knowledge, and the Rationalization of Teaching: A Genealogy of the Movement to Professionalize Teaching. *Harvard Educational Review*. Volume 62, Number 2: pp. 123–134.

Ladson-Billings, G. (1999). Preparing teachers for diverse student populations: A critical race theory perspective. *Review of Research in Education*, 24, 211–248.

———— (1995). *It's never too late to turn back: A critical race approach to multicultural education*. Paper presented at the annual meeting of the American Educational Research Association, San Francisco, April 18–22. (This paper contains portions of previously written work by Ladson-Billings, G.and Tate, W. F.).

Bibliography

Lather, P. (2004). Ethics Now: White Woman Goes to Africa and Loses Her Voice. Paper presented at the *American Educational Research Association* (San Diego, California; April 12–16, 2004).

—— (2001a). Getting Lost: Feminist Efforts Toward a Double(d) Science. Paper presented at the *Annual Meeting of the American Educational Research Association*. Seattle, Washington (College of Education, The Ohio State University, Columbus, Ohio).

—— (2001b). Applied Derrida: (Mis)Reading the work of Mourning in Educational Research. Paper presented at the *Annual Journal of Curriculum Theorizing Conference*, Bergamo, Ohio (College of Education, The Ohio State University, Columbus, Ohio).

—— (2001c). Postmodernism, poststructuralism and post(critical) ethnography. In P. Atkinson and S. Delamont (Eds.), *The Handbook of Ethnography*. (London, United Kingdom: Sage), pp. 477–492.

—— (1998). Against Empathy, Voice and Authenticity. Paper presented at the *American Educational Research Association (AERA) Annual Meeting*, March, 1998, San Diego, California.

—— (1996). Troubling Clarity: The Politics of Accessible Language. *Harvard Educational Review*. Volume 66, Number 3: pp. 525–545.

—— (1994). Critical Inquiry in Qualitative Research: Feminist and Poststructural Perspectives: Science after 'Truth'. In Ben Crabtree et al (eds.), *Exploring Collaborative Research in Primary Care*. (Thousand Oaks, California: Sage Publications), pp. 103–114.

—— (1991). *Getting smart: Feminist research and pedagogy with/in the postmodern.* New York, New York: Routledge.

—— (1998, March). *Against empathy, voice and authenticity.* Paper presented at the Annual Meeting of the American Educational Research Association. San Diego, California (College of Education, The Ohio State University, Columbus, Ohio).

—— (1986). Research as Praxis. *Harvard Educational Review*, 56(3), 257–277.

Lather, P and Smithies, C. (1997). *Troubling the Angels: Women Living with HIV/AIDS.* Boulder, Colorado; Westview/HarperCollins.

Lawrence, Richard. (1998). *School Crime and Juvenile Justice.* New York, New York; Oxford University Press.

Lincoln, Yvonna. (1998). From Understanding to Action: New Imperatives, New Criteria, New Methods for Interpretive Researchers. *Theory and Research in Social Education*, Volume 26, Number 1, 12–29.

Loadman, William, and Beverley Klecker. (1996). *Draft Evaluation of Professional Development Schools: A New School-University Partnership.* The College of Education, The Ohio State University and School Districts of Franklin County 1992–1995. Unpublished report.

Lorde, A. (1984). *Sister outsider: Essays and speeches by Audre Lorde.* Freedom, CA: The Crossing Press Feminist Series.

Lortie, D.C. (1975). *Schoolteacher-A Sociological Study.* Chicago, Illinois: University of Chicago Press.

Luke, Carmen. (1996). Feminist Pedagogy Theory: Reflections on Power and Authority. *Educational Theory*. Volume 46, Number 3: pp. 283–302.

Luke, C and Gore, J. (1992). *Feminism and Critical Pedagogy.* New York; Routledge.

MacCannell, D. (1994). *Empty meeting grounds: The tourist papers*. New York: Routledge.

McCoy, K. (1995) *Looking awry: A genealogical study of pre-service teacher encounters with popular media and multicultural education*. Columbus, Ohio: The Ohio State University. Unpublished dissertation.

McLaren, P. (1997). Decentering whiteness: In search of a revolutionary multiculturalism. *Multicultural Education*. Fall 1997: pp. 4–11.

Macedo, Donald (1998). English Only: The Tongue-Tying of America. In H. Svi Shapiro and David E. Purpel (eds.) *Critical Social Issues in American Education*. (Mahwah, New Jersey; Lawrence Erlbaum Associates), pp. 261–272.

McNeil, L. (2000). *Contradictions of School Reform: Educational Costs of Standardized Testing*. New York, New York; Routledge.

McRobbie, Angela. (1991). *Feminism and Youth Culture: From 'Jackie' to 'Just Seventeen'*. Boston, Massachusetts: Unwin Hyman.

McWilliam, Erica. (1999). *Pedagogical Pleasures*. Peter Lang; New York.

Marcus, George E., (1994). What Come (Just) After 'Post'?: The Case of Ethnography. In Denzin, Norma K., & Lincoln, Yvonna S. (Eds.), *Handbook of Qualitative Research*. (Thousand Oaks, California.: Sage Publications), pp. 563–574.

Marcus, George E., and Michael M.J. Fischer. (1986). *Anthropology as Cultural Critique: An Experimental Moment in the Human Sciences*. Chicago, Illinois: University of Chicago Press.

Marsh, C. and Willis, G. (1999). *Curriculum: Alternative Approaches, Ongoing Issues*. Upper Saddle River, New Jersey; Prentice Hall.

Marshall, Catherine and Rossman, Gretchen. (1995). *Designing Qualitative Research*. Thousand Oaks, California: Sage Publications.

Mazzei, L. (2004). Silent Listenings: Deconstructive Practices in Discourse-Based Research. *Educational Research*, Volume 33, Number 2: pp. 26–34.

Menand, Louis (2002). Faith, Hope and Clarity: September 11th and the American Soul. *The New Yorker*, September 16, 2002: pp. 98–104.

Michaelis, Karen L. (1999). Intersections of Critical Legal Theories: In Search of a Critical Theory of Juvenile Justice. Paper presented at the *American Educational Research Annual Conference (AERA)*, Montreal, Quebec, Canada, April 29–23, 1999.

Miller, J. L. 1990. *Creating spaces and finding voices: Teachers collaborating for empowerment*. Albany, NY: State University of New York.

Miller, Darcy, Catherine Trapani, Kathy Fejes-Mendoza, Carolyn Eggleston, and Donna Dwiggins (1999). 'Adolescent Female Offenders: Unique Considerations.' *Adolescence*, Volume 30, Number 118, Summer 1999: pp. 429–435. .

Miller, Darcy, Kathy Fejes-Mendoza, and Carolyn Eggleston (1997). Reclaiming 'Fallen Angels': Values and Skills for Delinquent Girls. *Reclaiming Children and Youth* Volume 5, Number 4, Winter 1997: pp. 231–234.

Mills, S. (1997). *Discourse*. New York, New York: Routledge.

Morrison, Keith, B. (2004). The Poverty of Curriculum Theory: a Critique of Wraga and Hlebowitsh. *Journal of Curriculum Studies*. Volume 36, Number 4: pp. 487–494.

Odem, Mary E. and Steve Schlossman (1991). Guardians of Virtue: The Juvenile Court and Female Delinquency in Early 20th-Century Los Angeles. *Crime and Delinquency*. Volume 37, Number 2, April 1991: pp. 186–203.

Ong, Aihwa (1999). Cultural Citizenship as Subject Making: Immigrants Negotiate Racial and Cultural Boundaries in the United States. In R. D. Torres, L. F. Miron and J. X. inda (eds.), *Race, Identity and Citizenship: A Reader*. (Malden, Massachusetts; Blackwell), pp. 262-294.

Ong, Aihwa. (1995). Women out of China: Traveling Tales and Traveling Theories in Postcolonial Feminism. In Ruth Behar and Deborah A. Gordon, (Eds.) *Women Writing Culture*. (Berkeley, California; University of California Press), pp. 360–372.

Osborne, P., and Segal, L. (1999). Interview with Stuart Hall: Culture and power. In R. D. Torres, L. F. Miron, and J. X. Inda (Eds.), *Race, Identity, and Citizenship: A Reader*. (Malden, Massachusetts: Blackwell), pp. 389–412.

Parry, Benita. (1995).Problems in Current Theories of Colonial Discourse. In Bill Ashcroft, Gareth Griffiths, and Helen Tiffin, (Eds.). *The Post-colonial Studies Reader*. (Reprint of Oxford Library Review 9, 1&2,1987). (New York, New York, Routledge), pp. 36–44.

Patton, Michael Quinn. (1990). *Qualitative Evaluation and Research Methods*. Newbury Park, Califnornia: Sage.

Petersen, Alan and Deidre Davies. (1997). Psychology and the Social Construction of Sex Differences in Theories of Aggression. *Journal of Gender Studies*. Volume 6, Number 3: pp. 309–319.

Pillow, W. (2000). Deciphering Attempts to Decipher Postmodern Educational Research. *Educational Researcher*, 29(5), 21–24.

Pinar, W.F. (2004). *What is Curriculum Theory?* Mahwah, New Jersey: Lawrence Erlbaum Associates.

——— (1998). *Curriculum: Toward New Identities*. New York, New York; Garland.

——— (1988). Autobiography and the architecture of the self. *The Journal of Curriculum Theorizing*. Volume 8, Number 1: pp. 7–36.

——— (1976). Self and Others. In W.F. Pinar and M.R. Grumet (1976) *Toward a Poor Curriculum* (Dubuque: Kendall Hunt), pp. 7–29.

Pinar, William F and Grumet, Madeleine R. (1976). *Toward a Poor Curriculum*. Dubuque, Iowa: Kendall Hunt.

Pinar, W.F., Reynolds, W.M., Slattery, P. and Taubman, P.M. (1995). *Understanding Curriculum*. New York, New York; Peter Lang.

Pitt, Alice. (1998). Qualifying Resistance: Some Comments on Methodological Dilemmas. *The International Journal of Qualitative Studies in Education*. Volume 11, Number 4: pp. 535–553.

Polkinghorne, Donald E. (1995). Narrative Configuration in Qualitative Analysis. In Amos J. Hatch and Richard Wisniewski, *Life History and Narrative*. (Washington, DC.; Falmer Press), pp. 5–24.

Popkewitz, T.S. (2000). The denial of change in educational change: Systems of ideas in the construction of national policy and evaluation. *Educational Researcher*, Volume 29, Number 2: pp. 17–29.

——— (1998a). *Struggling for the Soul: The Politics of Schooling and the Construction of the Teacher*. New York, NY: Teachers College Press.

——— (1998b). Knowledge, Power, and Curriculum: Revisiting a *TRSE* Argument. *Theory and Research in Social Education*. Winter 1998, Volume 26, Number 1: pp. 83–101.

———— (1998c). The Culture of Redemption and the Administration of Freedom as Research. *Review of Educational Research*, Spring 1998, Volume 68, Number 1: pp. 1–34.

———— (1998d). Dewey, Vygotsky, and the social administration of the individual: Constructivist pedagogy as systems of ideas in historical spaces. *American Educational Research Journal,* Volume 35, Number 4: pp. 535–570.

———— (1997) The production of reason and power: Curriculum history and intellectual traditions. *Journal of Curriculum Studies*. Volume 29, Number 2: pp. 131–164.

———— (1991). *A Political Sociology of Educational Reform: Power/Knowledge in Teaching, Teacher Education, and Research*. New York, New York: Teachers College Press.

Popkewitz, Thomas S., and Marie Brennan. (1998). Restructuring of Social and Political Theory in Education: Foucault and a Social Epistemology of School Practices. In Popkewitz, Thomas S. and Marie Brennan. (Eds.,) *Foucault's Challenge: Discourse, Knowledge, and Power in Education*. (New York, New York: Teachers College Press), pp. 3–35.

Popkewitz, Thomas S., and Hannu Simola. (1996). Professionalization, Academic Discourses and Changing Patterns of Power. In Popkewitz Thomas S., and Hannu Simola. (Eds.), *Professionalization and Education: A Research Report*. (Hakapaino Oy, Helsinki: Department of Teacher Education, University of Helsinki), pp. 7–146.

Pratt, Mary Louise. (1992). *Imperial Eyes: Travel Writing and Transculturation*. New York, New York: Routledge.

Prettyman, Sandra Spickard. (1998). "Discourses on Adolescence, Gender, and Schooling: An Overview." *Educational Studies: A Journal in the Foundations of Education*. Volume 29, Number 4, Winter 1998: pp. 329–40.

Rapp, D. (2002). Commentary—On lies, secrets, and silence: a plea to educational leaders. *The International Journal of Leadership in Education*. Volume 5, Number 2: pp. 175–185.

Readings, B. (1996). *The University in Ruins*. Cambridge, Massachusetts.: Harvard University Press.

Reynolds, W. M. and Weber, J. A. (Eds.,) (2004). Expanding Curriculum Theory: Dis/positions and Lines of Flight (Studies in Curriculum Theory). Mahwah, New Jersey; Lawrence Erlbaum Associates.

Richardson, L. (1997). *Fields of Play: Constructing an Academic Life*. New Brunswick, New Jersey: Rutgers University Press.

Rodriguez, Luis J. (1997). Hearts and Hands: A New Paradigm for Work with Youth and Violence. *Social Justice*. Winter 1997, Volume 24, Number 4: pp. 7–20.

Roman, L. (1993). Double Exposure. *Educational Theory*, 43(3), 279–308.

Rosaldo, R. (1999). Cultural citizenship, inequality, and multiculturalism. In R. D. Torres, L. F. Miron, and J. X. Inda (Eds.), *Race, Identity, and Citizenship: A Reader*. (Malden, Massachusetts: Blackwell), pp. 253–261.

Sarri, Rosemary. (1983). "Gender Issues in Juvenile Justice." *Crime and Delinquency*. July 1983, Volume 29, Number 3: pp. 381–397.

St. Pierre, E. A. (2002). "Science" Rejects Postmodernism. *Educational Researcher*, 31(8), 25–27.

———— (2000). The Call for Intelligibility in Postmodern Educational Research. *Educational Researcher. Volume* 29, Number 5: pp. 25–28.

Bibliography 149

St. Pierre, Elizabeth and Wanda Pillow. (2000). Introducing the Ruins. In St. Pierre, Elizabeth & Pillow, Wanda, (eds.), *Feminist Poststructural Theory and Practice in Education*. New York, NY: Routledge.

Savage, T.V. 1999. *Teaching self-control through management and discipline*. Boston, MA: Allyn & Bacon.

Schaffner, Laurie, Shelley Shick, and Nancy Stein (1997). Changing Policy in San Francisco: Girls in the Juvenile Justice System. *Social Justice*. Winter 1997, Volume 24, Number 4: pp. 187–211).

Schoonmaker, F., & Ryan, S. 1996. Does theory lead practice? Teachers' constructs about teaching: Top down perspectives. In J. Chafel & S. Reifel (Eds.), *Advances in early education and day care (vol. 8): Theory and practice in early childhood teaching*. (Greenwich, Connecticut: JAI Press), pp. 117–152.

Serres, Michel. (1993). *Angels: A Modern Myth*. New York, New York; Flammarion.

Serres, Michel with Bruno Latour. (1995). *Conversations on Science, Culture and Time*. Ann Arbor, Michigan: The University of Michigan Press.

Sheeler, K. K.H. 1996. *Mentors in the classroom, not just someone who can show you to your office: A brief summary of the literature*. ERIC Document Reproduction Service #ED406708

Sheriff, R.C., West, C., and Maschwitz, E. 1939. *Goodbye, Mr. Chips*. Los Angeles, California: MGM.

Shoicet, C.E. (2002) Education Department Report Calls for New Standards in Teacher-Training Programs, *The Chronicle of Higher Education*, 12 June.

Short, Edmund C. (Ed.), (1991). *Forms of Curriculum Inquiry*. Albany, New York: SUNY.

Simola, Hannu., Sakari Heikkinen and Jussi Silvonen. (1998). A Catalog of Possibilities: Foucaultian History of Truth and Education Research. In Popkewitz, Thomas S. and Brennan, Marie. (Eds.), *Foucault's Challenge: Discourse, Knowledge, and Power in Education*. (New York, New York: Teachers College Press), pp. 64–90.

Slattery, P., and Rapp, D. (2003). *Ethics and the Foundations of Education: Teaching Convictions in a Postmodern World*. Boston, Massachusetts; Allyn and Bacon.

Sleeter, C. (1994). White racism. *Multicultural Education*, Spring, 1994, 5–8, 39.

Slemon, Stephen. (1995). The Scramble for Post-colonialism. In Bill Ashcroft, Gareth Griffiths, and Helen Tiffin. (Eds.). *The Post-colonial Studies Reader*. (Reprint from Chris Tiffin and Alan Lawson (Eds.) De-Scribing Empire: Post-colonialism and Textuality. London, United Kingdom: Routledge, 1994). (New York, New York; Routledge), pp. 45–52.

Smith, John K. (1993). *After the Demise of Empiricism: The Problem of Judging Social and Educational Inquiry*. Norwood, New Jersey; Ablex Publishing Company.

Smith, Lesley Shacklady. (1978). Sexist Assumptions and Female Delinquency. In Carol Smart and Barry Smart (Eds.), *Women, Sexuality and Social Control*, (Boston, Massachusetts; Routledge and Kegan Paul), pp. 74–88.

Spark, Muriel. (1961). *The Prime of Miss Jean Brodie*. New York : HarperCollins.

Spivak, Gayatri (1995). Can the Subaltern Speak? In Bill Ashcroft, Gareth Griffiths and Helen Tiffin. (Eds.). *The Post-colonial Studies Reader*. (Reprinted from 1988 Cary Nelson and Lawrence Grossberg (eds.). Marxism and the Interpretation of Culture. London, MacMillan). (New York, New York; Routledge), pp. 24–28.

———— (1993). *Outside in the TeachingMachine*. New York, New York; Routledge.

Stanley, William B. (1992). *Curriculum for Utopia: Social Reconstructionism and Critical Pedagogy in the Postmodern Era*. New York, New York: State University of New York Press.

———— (1985). Recent research in the foundations of social education: 1976–1983. In W. B. Stanley (Ed.), *Review of Research in Social Studies Education* (pp. 309–390). Washington, DC: National Council for the Social Studies.

Steet, Linda (1999). Rescuing the Women Who Rescued the Girls: Those Other Public Schools. *Educational Foundations*. Spring 1999, Volume 13, Number 2: pp. 27–46.

Sullivan, Patricia A. (1996). Ethnography and the Problem of the 'Other.' In Peter Mortenson and Gesa E. Kirsch. (Eds.), *Ethics and Representation in Qualitative Studies of Literacy*. (Urbana, Illinois; National Council of Teachers of English), pp. 97–114.

Terry, Jennifer. (1991). "Theorizing Deviant Historiography". *Differences: A Journal of Feminist Cultural Studies*. Volume 3.2: pp. 55-74.

Tyler, L.L., and Goodlad, J.I. (1979). The personal domain: Curriculum meaning. In J.I. Goodlad (Ed.), *Curriculum inquiry: The study of curriculum practice*. (New York, New York: McGraw-Hill), pp. 191–208.

Usher, R. and Edwards, R. (1994). *Postmodernism and Education*. London; Routledge.

Valenzuela, A. (1999). *Subtractive Schooling: U.S.-Mexican Youth and the Politics of Caring*. New York, New York; SUNY Press.

Van Maanen, J. (1995). An end to innocence: The ethnography of ethnography. In J. Van Maanen. (Ed.), *Representation in ethnography* (Thousand Oaks, California: Sage), pp. 1–35.

———— (1988). *Tales of the Field*. Chicago, Illinois: The University of Chicago Press.

Villenas, S. (1996). The Colonizer/Colonized Chicana Ethnographer: identity, marginalization, and co-optation in the field. *Harvard Educational Review*. Volume 66, Number 4: pp. 711–731.

Visweswaran, Kamala. (1994). *Fictions of Feminist Ethnography*. Minneapolis, Minnesota: University of Minnesota Press.

Webber, Julie A. and Reynolds, William M. (2004). Afterword: Multiplicities and Curriculum Theory. In W. M. Reynolds and J. A. Webber. (Eds.), *Expanding Curriculum Theory: Dis/positions and Lines of Flight*. (Mahwah, New Jersey: LEA), pp. 203–209.

West, C. (1993). *Race Matters*. Boston: Beacon Press.

White, Jacquelyn, W. and Kowalski, Robin, M. (1994). Deconstructing the Myth of the Nonaggressive Woman: A Feminist Analysis. *Psychology of Women Quarterly*. Volume 18, Number 4, 1994: pp. 487–508.

Wynne, E.A., and Ryan, K. (1993). *Reclaiming our schools: A handbook on teaching character, academics, and discipline*. New York, New York: Maxwell Macmillan International.

Index

Alien, 3, 18, 109, 111, 112, 113, 114, 115, 116, 120, 121
Apple, 5, 63
Assimilationist, x, 97, 100, 101, 103, 104
Australia, ix, 114, 115

Bhabha, 11, 12, 13, 15, 46, 47, 48, 49, 81, 82, 94, 97, 99, 107, 109, 110, 116, 117, 119, 120 Britzman, 10, 11, 59, 68, 102, 103, 104, 111, 114, 126, 133, 134

Canada, ix, 23, 24, 115
Chesney-Lind, 86, 87, 88, 89, 93
Colonialism, 14
Colonized Knowing, 13, 49, 55, 83, 109
Counter-hegemonic, 6, 12, 36, 49, 61, 62, 99, 101, 109, 118
Critical Discourse Analysis, 15, 17, 18, 38, 40, 65, 82, 84, 85, 124
Crotty, 15, 16
Cultural Studies, ix, 85, 100
Curriculum Issues, xi, 120
Curriculum theory, x, xi, 1, 62, 135, 136, 139

Decolonized, 13
Democracy, ix, 4, 16, 61, 63, 67, 131
Deterritorialization, 12, 119
Dominant Culture, 114, 120

Ellsworth, 123, 125, 130, 131, 132
Equity, 20, 57, 59, 74, 81, 125
Erasure, 102, 110, 111, 125
Ethics, 25, 29, 39, 56, 57, 139
Essentialist, 7, 12, 21, 24, 27, 29, 36, 46, 48, 88, 100, 118, 133

Feminism, ix, 34
Feminized, x, 3, 13, 59, 67, 130, 133
Foucault, 2, 8, 9, 15, 17, 18, 36, 60, 63, 64, 78, 83, 84, 104, 106, 116, 117, 126, 137

Goodson, 24, 25, 27, 31
Hemegonic, 5, 79, 97, 100, 104, 112, 118, 124, 136
Home, x, xii, 12, 13, 14, 42, 46, 73, 75, 82, 83, 85, 90, 91, 95, 96, 97, 98, 109, 117, 118, 119, 120
Homeless (Homelessness), 12, 83, 95, 97, 110, 119, 120

Immigration, 48, 103, 111, 114, 121
Interpretivist, 135

Justice By Gender, 81, 84, 85, 94, 95, 97

Labaree, 66, 67, 68, 70, 116
Lather, 1, 2, 6, 15, 16, 30, 31, 32, 33, 40, 54, 55, 68, 115, 125, 126, 134, 137
Lincoln, 5, 6, 25, 60, 61, 64, 65, 79, 99

McWilliam, 126, 130
Masculinizing, 82, 91
Multicultural Education, x, 3, 61, 64, 79, 81, 98, 101, 102, 104, 105

Narrative, 6, 9, 14, 25, 26, 27, 28, 29, 31, 32, 34, 35, 41, 42, 48, 51, 52, 54, 55, 56, 98, 109, 111
Normalized, 2, 11, 31, 62, 63, 69, 78, 87, 97, 111, 125, 129, 133

Ong, 12, 98, 104, 111, 112, 120
Ontology, 15, 25, 45

Pillow, 53, 54, 55, 56, 138
Pinar, 1, 29, 71, 135, 136, 138, 139
Popkewitz, 4, 8, 9, 20, 24, 29, 31, 32, 37, 38, 55, 59, 60, 61, 62, 63, 64, 65, 66, 67, 69, 71, 76, 78, 79, 82, 86, 99, 104, 105, 106, 111, 112, 113, 116, 123, 126, 131, 139
Positivist, 25, 27, 68, 137
Postcolonial, ix, xi, 1, 6, 8, 11, 12, 13, 14, 15, 31, 52, 107, 113, 114, 136

Postmodern Moment, 5, 24, 29, 47, 61, 108
Poststructural ix, 1, 2, 8, 15, 16, 27, 29, 30, 31, 38, 60, 61, 62, 99, 114, 136
Psychoanalytic, ix, 1, 8, 10, 15, 38, 130, 136
Race, xi, 3, 20, 48, 54, 55, 56, 57, 60, 73, 74, 81, 98, 99, 100, 101, 102, 103, 104, 105, 110, 112, 115, 117, 121, 123, 124, 125, 131
Realist, 5, 7, 15, 25, 26, 27, 28, 29, 30, 35, 39, 40, 41, 42, 43, 45, 46, 48, 51, 55, 61, 65, 70, 74, 87, 99, 124, 131, 133
Regimes of Truth, 6, 8, 20, 63, 82, 85, 88, 91, 92, 93, 97, 100, 105, 115
Roman, 54
Rosaldo, 103, 111, 112
St. Pierre, 1, 56, 136, 137, 138
Serres, 7, 8, 17, 28, 29, 30, 45, 46
Sexualized Knowing, xi, 20, 55, 123
Social Studies, ix, x, 33, 35, 37, 38, 63
Slattery, 109, 139
Spivak, 13, 14, 84, 107, 116, 117
Subject Position, x, xi, 3, 10, 15, 16, 20, 57, 60, 62, 72, 81, 84, 85, 87, 91, 95, 96, 107, 111, 112, 113, 116, 124, 125, 129, 130, 133
Stanley, 16, 61, 62, 64
Steet, 87, 89, 96

Total Institutions, 2, 8, 65, 81, 83, 89, 96, 114

Villenas, 53, 55, 73
Visweswaran, 6, 12, 19, 25, 27, 28, 39, 40, 41, 43, 82, 119

White, x, 8, 53, 55, 57, 77, 88, 92, 100, 101, 102, 124
Whiteness, 3, 50, 60, 98, 99, 101, 102, 105

COMPLICATED

A BOOK SERIES OF CURRICULUM STUDIES

This series employs research completed in various disciplines to construct textbooks that will enable public school teachers to reoccupy a vacated public domain—not simply as "consumers" of knowledge, but as active participants in a "complicated conversation" that they themselves will lead. In drawing promiscuously but critically from various academic disciplines and from popular culture, this series will attempt to create a conceptual montage for the teacher who understands that positionality as aspiring to reconstruct a "public" space. *Complicated Conversation* works to resuscitate the progressive project—an educational project in which self-realization and democratization are inevitably intertwined; its task as the new century begins is nothing less than the intellectual formation of a public sphere in education.

The series editor is:

> Dr. William F. Pinar
> Department of Curriculum Studies
> 2125 Main Mall
> Faculty of Education
> University of British Columbia
> Vancouver, British Columbia V6T 1Z4
> CANADA

To order other books in this series, please contact our Customer Service Department:

> (800) 770-LANG (within the U.S.)
> (212) 647-7706 (outside the U.S.)
> (212) 647-7707 FAX

Or browse online by series:

> www.peterlang.com